soulful, savory, spicy, slurpy

MIKE LE and **STEPHANIE LE**

Creators of *i am a food blog*

Photography by MIKE LE

WORKMAN PUBLISHING · NEW YORK

Library of Congress Cataloging-in-Publication Data
Names: Le, Michael, author, photographer. | Le, Stephanie, author.
Title: That noodle life : soulful, savory, spicy, slurpy / Michael Le and
    Stephanie Le, creators of Iamafoodblog ; photography by Michael Le.
Identifiers: LCCN 2021007904 | ISBN 9781523505326 (hardcover) |
    ISBN 9781523505326 (ebook)
Subjects: LCSH: Cooking (Pasta) | Noodles. | LCGFT: Cookbooks.
Classification: LCC TX809.M17 L424 2021 | DDC 641.82/2—dc23
LC record available at https://lccn.loc.gov/2021007904

Design by Michael Le and Stephanie Le

Workman books are available at special discounts when purchased in bulk for premiums and sales promotions as well as for fundraising or educational use. Special editions or book excerpts can also be created to specification. For details, contact the Special Sales Director at the address below or send an email to specialmarkets@workman.com.

Workman Publishing Co., Inc.
225 Varick Street
New York, NY 10014-4381
workman.com

WORKMAN is a registered trademark of Workman Publishing Co., Inc.

Printed in South Korea
First printing February 2022

10 9 8 7 6 5 4 3 2 1

On Noodles

Noodles can mean different things to different people. For some, they are a comforting bowl of chicken noodle soup; for others, they're a crazy-exotic spice bomb. They can be a quick weeknight dinner or a 48-hour multicomponent undertaking. A bowl of noodles can instantly transport you to happy childhood memories or distant lands. A plate of pasta can be just like Mom used to make it—or it can be the restaurant dish of your year. There are many ways to interpret noodles, but among them is one universal constant: Noodles make people happy.

Whether they are long or short, loopy or straight, noodles may be one of the most common food items in the world. Nearly every culture has a celebrated homegrown noodle dish—from macaroni to fideos, from udon to pho—meaning there's a very good chance that most of us have tucked into a heap of incredible noodles at some point. And, thanks to the recent invention of instant noodles (or instant ramen, or pot ramen, or any of the hundred other names used to describe those dehydrated, super-quick noods), a huge number of us have probably enjoyed the exact same kind of noodles. In short, noodles unite us.

For the two of us, there's no question that noodles are our favorite food. We love noodles so much that we've stood in line for three hours in the middle of December in Tokyo for tsukemen, and we've braved the harsh Italian summer sun for authentic tagliatelle Bolognese. We've spent countless hours perfecting our homemade pasta and long, late nights figuring out just the right ratio of flour to water for our ramen noodles. There's no other food for which we've gone to such lengths. It wouldn't be a stretch to say that we've traveled a lot of the world in search of authentic and amazing noodles.

Writing this book meant that we've spent years thinking only about noodles. For months we lived, breathed, and, most importantly, ate noodles of all kinds. This book is chock-full of the tips, tricks, and techniques that we discovered as a result of our (un)healthy obsession—as well as the things we've picked up in our more than ten years immersed in the professional food world.

Good noodles come from the heart. Noodles are about having fun with your food, slurping the long ones and scooping the short ones and smiling as you eat. Good noodles are about the little details, the toppings, the work that's gone into the broth or sauce. Noodles are a tiny universe on your table.

We've spent long hours thinking about how to make this book easy and fun to use, and yet somehow also a master class in noodles. We've luxuriated in pages and pages of noodle notes, ingredient guides, and from-scratch noodle-making techniques. If you read and cooked this book from beginning to end, you would be, if not a noodle master, at least a seasoned noodle pro. We hope that by the end of this book, you'll be able to throw together an amazing fresh-from-scratch pasta dish (like our Over-the-Top Bolognese with Pappardelle, page 201, pappardelle and all), or create your own seasonally inspired ramen (Super Creamy Chicken Miso Ramen, page 221), or impress your friends by making Chinese take-out classics (Spicy Sesame Chili Oil Noodles, page 55) in less time than it takes for delivery. We want this book to make you fall deeper in love with noodles.

There's not nearly enough space in this book to cover all the noodles in the world, so instead we've focused on our very best and most beloved dishes. There are recipes from places we've visited and those we've invented and refined over years and years. Sometimes these recipes are quick and easy, and sometimes they are long and labor intensive, but we know they are rock solid and reliable, and they are—we think—always worth the time invested. We've meticulously tested and retested these recipes, changing ingredients and adjusting steps to make sure they're the best noodle recipes we could create. Where possible, in addition to providing a recipe for a traditional dish, we've also shown the building blocks of it (you'll find these "components" pages in the "Hello, My Name Is" sections throughout the book) so you can riff off our ingredient choices and make the dish your own. We really hope you give these recipes a try, make some noodles from scratch, and live your best noodle life.

—MIKE AND STEPH

No Noodles, No Life

In this book, we suggest a lot of different types and shapes of noodles. While we always aim to match the ideal shape to each dish, sometimes you need to make a substitution, and that's perfectly fine. Our recommendation is to try to swap like for like: wheat noodles for wheat noodles and rice noodles for rice noodles, short pasta for short pasta, long for long, and so on. For best results, try to use the same general shape; for example, if a recipe calls for curly fusilli bucati, swap in spiral-y rotini. For a lot of the longer Asian rice noodles, gluten-free spaghetti will work great. If noodle names are as mysterious to you as they once were (and sometimes still are) to us, refer to the handy visual reference on the following page.

What Is a Noodle?

Since beginning our noodle journey, we have asked almost everyone we know: What is a noodle? Their answers invariably support the notion that noodles are long and made of dough. Ramen, yes, and spaghetti too, because pasta is a noodle for sure. Then we ask, "What about macaroni or rotini? Are those not noodles, too?" *Yes, yes,* our friends nod emphatically, *short noodles are noodles, too.* After a little gentle pushing, everyone agrees: Noodles can be long *or* short. However, once we get into questions like "Is a dumpling a noodle?" things get more complex. The automatic answer is no . . . but then people get to thinking about how dumpling wrappers are often made of the same dough that's used to make noodles. So are dumplings *stuffed* noodles? Well, ravioli are also stuffed, and everyone agrees that ravioli count as pasta and pasta is a noodle, so that means ravioli are noodles as well, and we definitely consider wontons a noodle (see page 162). Other dumplings, though, seem very *un-noodley,* and that's where it breaks down. Between the two of us, we can't even agree on spaetzle and gnocchi, and we haven't even gotten into noodles made from shrimp and vegetables. Will we ever be able to define what a noodle is? Maybe we don't have to. Maybe we all know a noodle when we see one. After all, the noodle universe is wide and the noodle gods are forgiving.

A HAIKU GUIDE TO NOODLES

Bucatini
Long, dense, hollow tubes
Like spaghetti with a hole
Sub with spaghetti

Casarecce
Short S-shaped pasta
Hard to spell, easy to eat
Sub with rotini

Calamarata
Squid-shaped pasta rings
Pairs perfectly with seafood
Sub rigatoni

Chow Mein
You know what this is
You'd order it every night
Sub with spaghetti

Fusilli Bucati
Looks like a phone cord
(Do kids even know that shape?)
Sub with rotini

Instant Noodles
A flash-fried noodle
Much more common than pasta
No subs required

Linguine
Like flat spaghetti
Wide surface perfect for sauce
Sub with spaghetti

Chinese Oil Noodles
Fresh thick egg noodles
Look like ramen, called lo mein
Sub with spaghetti

Mafalda
Tiny lasagna
Comes in both short and long forms
Sub with rotini

Mezze Rigatoni
Like rigatoni
But a cute shorter version
Sub big-atoni

Pappardelle
Store-bought or handmade
Like wide tagliatelle
Sub widest pasta

Radiatori
Radiator shape
Many ridges to catch sauce
Sub with rotini

Ramen
Long and slurpable
Beloved across the world
Sub with spaghetti

Rice Stick
A flat rice noodle
Often for pho or stir-fried
You'll find it online

Soba
Long strands of buckwheat
Look for few ingredients
Sub with whole wheat spag

Spaghettoni
Bigger is better
Satisfyingly thicker
Sub with spaghetti

Tagliatelle
Flat strands of pasta
Bolognese's classic shape
Sub fettuccine

Udon
Thick and chewy strands
The best ones are found frozen
Asian stores have them

Rice Vermicelli
A round rice noodle
Thick or thin, still gluten free
Sub with spaghetti

Ziti
Smooth tubes of pasta
Available long or short
Substitute penne

How to Noodle

We've tried our best to make this book super easy to dive right into, with no pantry recipes or ingredient selections up front, but there are some small key things to know before you start noodling.

Fresh vs. Dried vs. Frozen

Most people tend to assume that fresh handmade noodles are somehow fancier and thus tastier than dried noodles, and that discount dried pastas or noodles are second-class noodle citizens. But this is a misperception. A high-quality dried pasta will taste better than a poorly made fresh pasta any day. Judging the quality of dried pasta is easy. Good pasta has a rough, almost sandpaper-like texture. This makes it better at picking up sauce and flavor than commercial pastas with a smooth surface. Look for the words "bronze-extruded" on the package.

Frozen noodles are a good alternative to dried, especially when it comes to Asian noodles. Often these noodles have a superior texture to their dried counterparts while still being commercially available and of consistent quality. When it comes to udon and ramen, frozen is actually the only choice we'll consider unless we are making the noodles ourselves.

We love both fresh and dried noodles and use them interchangeably. You can too—just make sure to account for the weight difference when portioning. Our dry noodle recipes are portioned out at 3 ounces (uncooked) per person and our fresh at 6 ounces. In A Haiku Guide to Noodles (see page x), you can see the different noodles we use in this book and easy-to-find substitutes.

Whether it's pasta, ramen, or rice noodles, though, commercial noodles also have the advantage of being tested and reliable—if the package says they're al dente in 7 minutes, they most likely will be al dente in 7 minutes. Artisanal or fresh noodles tend to need a bit more babysitting while they cook. Our rule with these is to pay close attention to the pot and take out the pasta as soon as it floats. Nothing is sadder than a soggy, overcooked noodle.

Asian Noodles

Asian noodles don't come in the same variety of shapes as Italian pastas, but don't be fooled—each noodle is vastly different based on how it was made, its thickness and shape, and its ingredients. Whether buckwheat soba, hand-torn noodles, or pho, there can be hundreds of noodle choices, dried and fresh. We cover the major varieties used in this book on page x and suggest substitutions if you can't easily find them.

Perfect Pasta Water

Don't forget to salt your pasta water. Most Italian pastas (including our recipe for homemade pasta on page 12) don't actually contain salt, so salting the water is the key to flavorful noodles. A popular rule of thumb is to salt the water until it tastes like the ocean. We diverge from that advice here, since almost all of our pastas are finished with a generous amount of starchy pasta water—oversalting the water could lead to an over-seasoned sauce. A large pinch of salt per quart of water will suffice.

Most Asian noodles are salted and their accompanying sauces tend to be on the strong side, so we don't salt our water when making Asian noodles.

Using a Timer

When cooking noodles, we use a timer religiously, and we recommend you do, too. Even when cooking pastas and noodles with no time listed on the package, we set the timer to track how long it takes the noodle to cook to our liking, so we can repeat it every time.

Adding Noodles to Boiling Water

Always allow your water to come to a rolling boil before adding the noodles. Adding noodles to water that hasn't yet hit a boil will yield undercooked noodles or soggy, overcooked ones. Start your timer the moment the noodles hit the water.

The Deal with al Dente

These days, everyone seems to know to cook pasta al dente, but *al dente* means different things to different people. The original meaning of the phrase comes from the Italian for "to the teeth" and implies that the pasta is still slightly firm when bitten; in the case of spaghetti, for instance, there should still be the tiniest speck of white in the center. To many people, this seems undercooked—first-time visitors to Italy often complain that the pasta is too firm and tastes starchy—but after eating al dente pasta long enough, you begin to crave that firmness. With all noodles, try cooking them for a little less time than what's recommended on the package and going a little firmer to find what texture you really love. You can always throw the noodles back in the saucing pan or let them sit in the soup a little longer if you find they're too firm.

Unless a recipe states otherwise, we stop cooking our pasta a few minutes before it's al dente and finish it in the sauce. We cook Asian noodles right to the package time.

Soaking

Precooked noodles (such as Chinese oil noodles or chow mein) and noodles that will be fried (such as frozen udon) don't need to be boiled or cooked. Just soak them in a large bowl filled with hot tap water for a minute or two to warm them up, then swish them around a bit to loosen them up.

Draining

Most of the recipes in this book call for draining the noodles well (and for pastas, often reserving the cooking water, too). This is the golden rule for Asian noodles, but the truth is that when it comes to pasta, the word "drain" is a touch misleading—we rarely drain our pasta using a colander. Instead, we prefer to use tongs or a strainer spoon to scoop it out and transfer it to the saucepan—any water that clings to the noodles helps emulsify everything into a creamy, glossy sauce (see page xix). As a bonus, that leaves behind an entire pot of hot, starchy cooking water that can be added to the sauce as needed to help it hug the pasta. So when you're instructed to "drain well," you can either reserve the water as directed and pour the noodles into a colander or use tongs/a strainer spoon to pull them from the water. Choose whichever method you prefer; we won't judge.

Rinsing

It bears repeating: Never rinse your pasta. You're washing away all the starch that will help the sauce cling to it. The exceptions here are rice noodles, lasagna noodles, and noodles for cold salads—essentially, if the noodles won't be sauced or souped immediately, you'll need to give them a rinse or you'll end up with a solid, inseparable mass. Otherwise, don't rinse your noods! And oiling your pasta? Don't. That will make the sauce slide right off. If you've ever wondered why pastas in restaurants always seem richer than homemade, this is one reason.

Bowls for Soup Noodles

Time and time again we've heard from friends that they made our soup noodle recipes, only to realize they had no bowls in which to serve them. Our soup recipes call for bowls that have a 3- to 4-cup capacity, which means they should be about 9 inches wide and 3½ inches deep. You don't need to get fancy—even mixing bowls will do—but be sure to have enough on hand before serving that gorgeous beef pho (page 141) or Taiwanese noodle soup (page 143) that you spent hours on.

Warming Soup Noodle Bowls

If you want the ultimate in luxury, don't forget to warm your soup noodle bowls. Much like how restaurants warm plates to keep food hot and fresh, warming noodle bowls ensures that when the bowl gets to the table, everything is piping hot. Soups are extremely good at transferring the cold from the bowl to themselves, so warming your bowl is a simple step that will take your home noodling to restaurant level.

Here's how: Turn your tap on as hot as it will go and fill the noodle bowls almost to the brim. Let sit for at least 3 minutes. When ready to serve, just pour the water out. Your bowls will be toasty and warm—and your soup will stay that way, too.

Toppings

Toppings are often the key differentiator between an average bowl of noodles and an incredible one. They offer variations in taste, pops of flavor, and crunch or crisp between slurps. In these recipes, we suggest toppings that are easy to buy or prepare. They are generally optional, but we highly suggest that you go the distance and make sure to include toppings with each recipe you make. You'll see them called out in sidebars throughout the book.

Eating Immediately

It should go without saying, but all noodle and pasta dishes benefit from being eaten right away. Cold pasta that's sat too long on the countertop can be congealed and unappetizing. Cold soup noodles can be a soggy mess. We won't let this happen to you—our recipes are written so that the final assembly step happens in minutes, allowing you to wait until everyone is ready to eat before saucing that pasta or plating those noodles. Bonus: The finished dishes look that much more impressive—and you look much more chef-y—when you have all your ducks in a row, ready to go, and expertly prepare each plate in moments.

Saucing is the single biggest difference between home-cooked and restaurant-level pasta.

Properly seasoning and saucing your pasta will make a bigger difference to your final dish than sweating over a long simmer. Here's how.

Pasta Water Is Gold

Although you'll hear that your pasta water should be as salty as the ocean, we try to stay a little on the conservative side: Since we use pasta water to finish many of our sauces, we want to make sure the resulting sauce isn't overseasoned. For us, 1 large pinch of salt per 4 cups water is about right.

We said it before, don't rinse (or oil) your noodles! The starch left behind on the noodles helps pick up sauce and flavor. We go a little further in our kitchen and don't drain the noodles either. Instead, we transfer them directly to the warm sauce using soft silicone tongs or a strainer spoon (see page 243). That leaves behind a whole pot of starchy pasta water for us to use as needed.

Sauce as You Go

Most of the recipes in this book yield two to four portions. If you are making a recipe that yields more sauce than you will eat right away, cook less pasta and sauce it as needed: Go with ¼ cup sauce per portion of pasta for oil-based sauces, and ½ cup per portion of pasta for all other sauces. Store or freeze any remaining sauce.

Undercook Your Pasta

Undercooking your pasta means you can finish the pasta in the sauce without worrying about mushy noodles. We cook dried pasta 2 to 3 minutes less than the time indicated to al dente on the package. We remove fresh pasta from the cooking water as soon as it floats.

Finish Cooking the Pasta in the Sauce

While your pasta is cooking, transfer the appropriate portion of sauce from the sauce pot to a large nonstick skillet and bring it up to a bare simmer. Add your undercooked pasta along with about 2 tablespoons per portion of the reserved pasta water. Turn up the heat and gently stir and toss, simmering everything together so that the pasta cooks and the sauce is thick and glossy and clings to the noodles. If the pasta gets too dry, add more of the pasta water, a little at a time.

Cozy

NOODS FOR COZY MOODS

COMFORT NOODLES

Whether you're having a good day or a bad one, noodles are there for you.

They can distract and delight and, best of all, they don't care what you look like. If you want noodles first thing in the morning or in the middle of the afternoon or at 3 a.m., go for it—noodles never judge. The best comfort noodles are those that impart a sense of nostalgia. Maybe you grew up eating mac and cheese that your mom made. Maybe your grandpa makes an excellent sesame soy Shanghai noodle stir-fry loaded with vegetables. Maybe Drunk You has sought solace in a can of ravioli. Whatever your comfort noodle, you're sure to find something to fit the bill here. From Super Spaghetti and Meatballs (page 33) to Extra Rich, Extra Egg Yolk Mezze Rigatoni Carbonara (page 21), these recipes will have you feeling like everything is right with the world.

This is a classic Italian Sunday sauce. There's nothing fancy about it; it's just an easy, lazy sauce that tastes incredible with tagliatelle (or really any kind of pasta) and requires almost no prep, especially if you own a food processor. Cook it as long or as quickly as your hunger allows—it will fill the house with the wonderful aromas of meat, wine, tomato, and cheese. Like most traditional sugos, this sauce combines different kinds of ground meat. If you can't find one or the other, feel free to go with just one.

REALLY SAVORY SUNDAY SAUCE

SLOW-BRAISED SUGO WITH TAGLIATELLE

2 tablespoons olive oil

4 ounces guanciale, chopped

1 clove garlic, peeled and thinly sliced

2 tablespoons chopped carrot

½ small onion, peeled and chopped

½ pound ground pork

¼ pound ground veal or beef

Salt and freshly ground black pepper

¼ cup tomato paste

1 cup dry white wine

1 cup whole milk, plus extra as needed

1 bay leaf

1 tablespoon dried oregano

½ cup finely grated Parmigiano-Reggiano cheese

12 ounces dried tagliatelle

1. Combine the oil, guanciale, and garlic in a large pot over medium-high heat. Cook, stirring, until the garlic becomes fragrant, 1 to 2 minutes. Add the carrot and onion and cook, stirring occasionally, until the carrot is soft and the onion is translucent, about 5 minutes. Add the ground meats and cook, stirring, until browned, 8 to 10 minutes. Season to taste with salt and pepper, then add the tomato paste and cook until the flavors meld and the sauce reduces slightly, 2 minutes.

2. Add the wine, stirring and scraping the bottom of the pan to release any browned bits. Let simmer until reduced by half, 5 to 6 minutes, then add 1 cup of the milk, the bay leaf, oregano, and Parmigiano.

3. Reduce the heat to a bare simmer and let cook, partially covered and stirring occasionally, until the flavors meld and the sauce becomes a pale pink, at least 30 minutes and up to 4 hours. If the sauce gets too dry, stir in more milk, ¼ cup at a time. Taste and adjust the seasoning, and discard the bay leaf.

4. Bring a large pot of salted water to a boil over high heat. Add the tagliatelle and cook according to the package directions until it is 3 minutes shy of al dente. Drain well, reserving 1 cup of the pasta cooking water.

5. Return the tagliatelle to the pot and add the sauce. Cook over medium heat until the tagliatelle is al dente and coated with the sauce, about 3 minutes. If the sauce seems too thick, add reserved pasta water ¼ cup at a time to thin it. Serve hot.

Serves 4

Toppings

Finely grated Parmigiano
Flaky sea salt
Crushed red pepper flakes
Freshly cracked black pepper

Make It Ahead

This sauce will keep in an airtight container in the refrigerator for 3 to 4 days (it gets better over time!). To serve, simply reheat the sauce and toss it with freshly cooked pasta.

The truth is, we used to not love soba. It always came in third place in the Japanese noodle pantheon, after ramen and udon. Then we had really good soba in Japan and things changed. Good soba has a delicate subtlety to it—it's all about the nuttiness of the buckwheat flour and the texture of the noodles. For anyone who doesn't love soba (yet), this is our gateway recipe: Cold soba gets tossed with a simple dressing made from dashi, soy, mirin, and bonito. The noodles are the star—try to find soba that is mostly buckwheat, which is what gives soba its aroma and nuttiness. Also, don't forget to slurp; it's part of the soba experience.

THE SOBA BOWL

REALLY PRETTY SOBA WITH CUCUMBER AND AVOCADO

½ cup dashi
(see page 236)

2 tablespoons soy sauce
(preferably Japanese)

2 tablespoons mirin

¼ cup bonito flakes
(see page 237)

2 bundles (6 ounces
each) dried soba

¼ English cucumber,
trimmed and thinly
sliced

2 avocados, pitted,
peeled, and sliced

¼ cup thinly sliced green
onions

Microgreens, for serving
(optional)

1. Combine the dashi, soy, and mirin in a small saucepan and bring to a simmer over medium heat. Remove from the heat and add the bonito flakes. Let soak for 5 minutes, then strain through a sieve into a large bowl; discard the bonito flakes.

2. Cook the soba according to the package directions and rinse thoroughly in cold water. Drain the soba well and add the noodles to the dressing in the bowl. Toss to coat.

3. Plate the soba and arrange the cucumber, avocado, and green onions on top, dividing them evenly. Top with microgreens, if using. Serve.

Serves 4

5x Better

Top each bowl with nori seaweed strips, a dab of wasabi paste, and some toasted sesame seeds.

 tip! Switch out the vegetables to make this your own. Some ideas: thinly sliced sweet bell peppers, shredded cabbage or lettuce, corn kernels, sliced red onions, sliced carrots, sliced radishes, chopped green beans, thinly sliced fennel, and/or chopped fresh parsley, dill, mint, basil, or tarragon.

Amatriciana is a simple and slightly spicy tomato sauce enhanced by rich and fatty cured pork in the form of guanciale. Red pepper flakes add just the right amount of heat, and sharp, salty sheep's milk pecorino finishes the show. Although you don't typically add any aromatics to amatriciana sauce, here the onion and garlic round out and balance the flavors.

ALL-IN AMATRICIANA

PORK, PECORINO, AND CHITARRA

Serves 2

Toppings

Freshly cracked black
  pepper
Finely grated pecorino
Crushed red pepper
  flakes

tip!

Guanciale, cured unsmoked pork jowl, is a great item to keep socked away in the fridge because you can get a large piece of it for not much money and it keeps for a long time. If necessary, you can sub pancetta or even bacon (though the latter will be smoky).

3 ounces guanciale, chopped

½ small onion, peeled and finely chopped

1 clove garlic, peeled and pressed or minced

½ teaspoon freshly ground black pepper

¼ teaspoon crushed red pepper flakes

1 cup canned crushed tomatoes

Salt

6 ounces dried chitarra or bucatini

1 cup finely grated pecorino Romano cheese

1. Place the guanciale in a large sauté pan over medium heat and cook, allowing the fat to render and the guanciale to brown and crisp, 4 to 6 minutes. Add the onion, garlic, ground black pepper, and red pepper flakes and cook until the onion is soft, 1 to 2 minutes. Stir in the tomatoes and bring to a simmer. When bubbles start to break the surface, reduce the heat to low and cook, stirring occasionally, until the sauce is slightly reduced, 15 to 20 minutes.

2. Meanwhile, bring a large pot of salted water to a boil over high heat. Add the chitarra and cook according to the package directions until it is 3 minutes shy of al dente. Drain well, reserving 1 cup of the pasta cooking water.

3. Transfer the chitarra to the sauce and cook over medium heat, stirring, until the sauce clings to the pasta and the pasta is al dente, 2 to 3 minutes. If the sauce seems too thick, add reserved pasta water ¼ cup at a time to thin it. Remove from the heat and add the pecorino, stirring until it is melted. Serve hot.

In Japan, you'll find tons of yakisoba stands at summertime festivals selling portions of thick, fried ramen noodles (not buckwheat soba, despite the name) in the hot summer heat. Yakisoba vendors can use up many whole heads of cabbage in a day, but since we're cooking on a smaller scale, we went with Brussels sprouts here—they are just like cabbages, but mini. We also switched out the traditional Japanese yakisoba noodles for easier-to-find spaghetti. It sounds weird but it works—one taste and you'll feel like you're in Japan.

FESTIVAL YAKISOBA

BACON AND BRUSSELS SPROUTS SOBA

Salt

6 ounces dried spaghetti

2 tablespoons Japanese Worcestershire sauce (see Note)

1 tablespoon oyster sauce

1 tablespoon ketchup

½ tablespoon soy sauce

½ tablespoon mirin

4 slices bacon (preferably thick cut)

½ cup thinly sliced leeks (rinsed if gritty)

1 small carrot, cut into matchsticks

½ cup thinly sliced Brussels sprouts

Freshly ground black pepper

1. Bring a large pot of salted water to a boil over high heat. Add the spaghetti and cook according to the package directions until it is al dente. Drain well.

2. Meanwhile, make the sauce: Whisk together the Worcestershire, oyster sauce, ketchup, soy sauce, and mirin in a small bowl. Set aside.

3. Cook the bacon in a large sauté pan over medium heat until the fat renders and the bacon is crispy, 4 to 6 minutes. Drain off excess bacon fat if there are more than 2 tablespoons in the pan. Add the leeks, carrot, and Brussels sprouts to the pan and cook, stirring occasionally, until slightly soft, 1 to 2 minutes.

4. Add the noodles to the pan, then the sauce, and toss until everything is evenly coated. Season with salt and pepper to taste. Serve hot.

Note: Japanese Worcestershire sauce is thicker and sweeter than regular Worcestershire. It's available in the international aisle of most large grocery stores, at Asian grocery stores, or online. If you can't find it, sub with 2 tablespoons of ordinary Worcestershire and 2 teaspoons of sugar.

Serves 2

Toppings

Sliced green onions
Nori seaweed strips
Pickled red ginger

5x Better

Try topping with high-quality bonito flakes (see page 237) for an extra-authentic hit of umami.

WHY & HOW YOU SHOULD MAKE

HOMEMADE PASTA

WITH A CHITARRA

It's the best spaghetti you'll ever have, and it looks nothing like what you get out of a box. Instead of those familiar round strands, think of a perfect square-sided noodle: just hefty enough, with rough, straight sides that are like a sponge for sauce.

You can make a multitude of pasta shapes from our standard pasta dough recipe, but our shape of choice is chitarra, a very old, very traditional square-cut spaghetti that comes from the Abruzzo region in Italy. It's made using a chitarra (Italian for "guitar"), a wooden frame with wires strung across it. Chitarra pasta cutters are easy to find online and go for $30 to $40. Look for an Italian-made wooden one with stainless steel strings.

Sheets of pasta are pressed and rolled over the strings, which cuts them into precise strands with perfectly squared-off edges. To loosen the strands of pasta from the wires, you gently strum the strings of the chitarra so the strands fall through the spaces into the little well at the bottom. Unlike most other fresh egg pastas, which tend to be tender and sort of silky, spaghetti alla chitarra has more of a bite to it. Once you taste it, you'll never go back to store-bought. (If you must, they actually *do* sell "square-cut spaghetti." But where's the fun in that?)

DOUBLE DOUBLE
SPAGHETTI ALLA CHITARRA

1 cup all-purpose flour, plus extra as needed (see Note)

1 large egg plus 1 large egg yolk

Salt

Note: The general rule for homemade pasta is 100 grams of flour per egg, but here we've just specified 1 cup because the truth is that the amount of flour is inexact. Depending on the humidity of your kitchen, how dry your hands are, what surface you use, and many other variables, you may need a lot more flour or a lot less. Shoot for a dough that's mostly dry yet still tacky before resting. As you become more experienced making pasta at home, you'll dial in a more precise measure that works for you.

1. Place the flour in a large bowl and make a well in the middle with your fingers. Drop the egg and egg yolk into the well and use a fork to whisk the eggs, slowly incorporating the flour little by little, until a dough starts to form.

2. Lightly flour a work surface and turn out the dough mixture onto it. Knead the dough until it is smooth and elastic, about 10 minutes, then wrap it with plastic wrap and let it rest at room temperature for 1 hour. (Alternatively, use a stand mixer fitted with a dough hook to knead the mixture until it forms a smooth, elastic dough.)

3. After the dough has rested, unwrap it, dust it lightly with flour on both sides, and lay it on a floured work surface. Using your hands, press it into a long rectangular shape about ½ inch thick. From here, you can either roll out the dough by hand using a rolling pin, or you can use a pasta machine to roll it out, starting at the widest setting and dialing it down after each pass through the machine. Roll the dough until it is ¹⁄₁₆ inch thick (on most pasta machines, this is setting #4).

4. To make spaghetti, we use the narrowly spaced side of the chitarra (we find the other side is useful for making thicker noodles or tagliatelle). Use a sharp knife to trim the

Makes 1 portion (but is infinitely scalable)

Continued on next page   ⟶

Make It Ahead

If you're not cooking
the pasta right away,
you can lightly dust
it with flour, place it
on a plate or tray, and
cover it with plastic
wrap. The uncooked
pasta will hold in the
fridge for 1 day (it will
become a little darker
in color).

pasta sheet 25 percent shorter than the length of the chitarra (usually about 8 inches),
then place the dough in the middle of the chitarra and use a rolling pin to push the dough
through the strings, cutting it into spaghetti. Shake out the strands of pasta, lightly dust
them with flour, and spread them out on a lightly floured surface and let dry slightly,
10 to 15 minutes. Repeat with the remaining dough.

5. To cook the spaghetti, bring a large pot of salted water to a boil over high heat. Add the
spaghetti and cook until it is al dente and just starting to float, 2 to 3 minutes. Taste to
ensure the pasta is cooked through. Reserve some of the pasta cooking water as directed
in the recipe for the finished dish, then drain well.

Variations

1 Tagliatelle

You can use the other side of the chitarra to cut the pasta sheet into tagliatelle,
or use a knife to cut it into ¼-inch-wide noodles. Cook as directed above for
3 to 4 minutes.

2 Pappardelle

We like our pappardelle wider than what you can find commercially. Roll the pasta
as thin as you can (or to setting #5 on most pasta machines) and cut it into 12-inch
lengths. Cut these sheets lengthwise into 4 slices, making extremely wide noodles.
Cook as directed above for 2 to 3 minutes.

3 Pici

This dough makes excellent pici—humble, simple, hand-rolled thick noodles. Pici
aren't perfect. Each noodle is different—thinner in some places, thicker in others.
They have a wonderfully chewy bite that stands up to hearty sauces (like our sugo,
page 5, or Luxe Lamb Ragu, page 105).

In Step 3, use a rolling pin to roll the dough until it is about ⅛ inch thick. Use a
large sharp knife to cut it into long strips ⅛ inch wide, then use your fingertips
or the palms of your hands against an unfloured work surface to roll the strips
of dough out into ropes about 12 inches long. Pici takes an especially long time
to cook to al dente. Cook as directed above, for 8 to 10 minutes (taste one—it
should be slightly firm, chewy, and cooked through).

Cacio e pepe literally translates to "cheese and pepper." When a dish has minimal ingredients like this one does, the flavor of each is paramount. It goes without saying that the cacio (pecorino Romano, always) should be freshly grated—but don't neglect the pepe. Freshly cracked black pepper is key—blooming it over low heat opens up the aromatic oils and infuses the sauce, making sure that the pepper flavor is present in the background and not just at the forefront as a finishing touch.

CACIO E PEPE

PICI WITH LOTS OF CHEESE AND CRACKED BLACK PEPPER

Salt

2 portions homemade pici (see page 14) or 6 ounces dried bucatini

2 tablespoons (¼ stick) unsalted butter (see Note)

2 teaspoons freshly cracked black pepper (see Tip)

2 cups finely grated pecorino Romano cheese

1. Bring a large pot of salted water to a boil over high heat. Add the pici and cook until it is just floating, about 7 minutes. (If you're substituting dried pasta, cook it according to the package directions until it is 3 minutes shy of al dente.) Drain well, reserving 1½ cups of the pasta cooking water.

2. Meanwhile, melt the butter in a large sauté pan over medium heat. Stir in the pepper and let bloom in the butter for 30 seconds. Add ¾ cup of the pasta water to the pan and bring it to a gentle boil over medium heat, whisking to emulsify the water and butter, about 1 minute. Add the pici to the pan and cook, tossing occasionally, until the pici is al dente and the sauce reduces and becomes thick and glossy, about 3 minutes.

3. Remove from the heat and gradually stir in the pecorino until it's melted. The sauce should be creamy; if it looks dry, add more of the pasta cooking water a tablespoon at a time to loosen it. Serve hot.

Note: We almost always use unsalted butter to better control the seasoning of our food, and in our opinion, the best option is grass-feed organic butter, ideally from Iceland, New Zealand, Canada, or a small local producer. (Try a little grass-fed butter and flaky sea salt on toast. If you've never had it before, it will blow your mind.)

 Loosen the little knob on top of your pepper grinder for a coarse pepper. For this recipe, you want the grind to be as coarse as possible.

Serves 2

Toppings

Finely grated pecorino
Freshly cracked black pepper
(When it comes to cacio e pepe, more is more!)

Why order in when you can stir-fry your own plateful of noodles in 20 minutes or less? There are a few ways to ensure a quality plate: A quick cornstarch and Shaoxing wine marinade for the pork helps tenderize it and improve browning; a mix of dark and light soy sauce adds color and saltiness; and searing the noodles on high heat adds a wok-fried smokiness even if you don't have a wok. You can find Shanghai noodles in the fresh noodle section at your local Asian grocery store or grab a package of frozen udon (both come precooked).

BETTER THAN TAKE OUT

FRIED SHANGHAI NOODLES WITH PORK BELLY AND KALE

Serves 4

Toppings

Sliced green onions
Crispy fried onions
  (see page 239)
Chili oil (preferably
  homemade; see
  page 53)

Note: If using frozen udon in Step 3, soak them until defrosted, 2 to 3 minutes.

2 tablespoons light soy sauce

2 teaspoons cornstarch

1 teaspoon Shaoxing wine (see page 235)

1 teaspoon sugar

½ pound pork belly, sliced into matchsticks

1 tablespoon dark soy sauce

1 tablespoon hoisin sauce

2 tablespoons sodium-free chicken stock

2 teaspoons toasted sesame oil

1 pound fresh traditional Shanghai thick noodles or frozen udon (see Note)

1 tablespoon neutral oil

1 bunch kale, stemmed and chopped

1. Combine 1 tablespoon of the light soy sauce with the cornstarch, Shaoxing wine, and sugar in a large bowl. Mix in the pork to coat thoroughly. Set aside.

2. Make the sauce: Combine the remaining 1 tablespoon light soy sauce with the dark soy sauce, hoisin sauce, chicken stock, and sesame oil in a small bowl. Set aside.

3. Fill a large bowl with hot tap water and add the noodles. Let soak until loosened and warmed through, 30 seconds to 1 minute. Drain and set aside.

4. Heat a large wok or skillet over medium heat. When the wok starts to smoke, add the neutral oil and swirl until shimmery. Add the pork with its marinade and cook, stirring occasionally, until it is golden brown and crispy, 3 to 5 minutes.

5. Add the kale and toss to combine. When the kale has wilted slightly, add the noodles and the sauce. Turn the heat up to high and toss to combine. Sear until everything is smoky and slightly charred, about 2 minutes. Serve hot.

 This basic fried noodle recipe is very versatile—you can use this technique and sauce with any combination of protein or veg. The sky's the limit.

Start this recipe off with room-temperature eggs and ditch the whites—egg whites and yolks cook at different temperatures, so an all-yolk carbonara is easier to control. Whisking the sauce in a large bowl gives you room to aerate the yolks, so they'll disperse evenly around your noodles. The egg yolk–cheese mixture will be thick, but the residual heat of the noodles and hot starchy pasta water will simultaneously cook the eggs *and* emulsify and loosen everything into a glossy sauce.

THE DOUBLE YOLK

EXTRA RICH, EXTRA YOLK MEZZE RIGATONI CARBONARA

4 large egg yolks, at room temperature (see Note)

1 cup finely grated Parmigiano-Reggiano cheese

1 cup finely grated pecorino Romano cheese

¼ teaspoon freshly ground black pepper

3 ounces guanciale, chopped

Salt

6 ounces dried mezze rigatoni

1. Whisk together 2 of the egg yolks with the Parmigiano, pecorino, and black pepper in a large bowl until combined. Set aside.

2. Cook the guanciale in a large sauté pan over medium heat, stirring occasionally, until the fat renders and the guanciale is browned and crisp, 4 to 6 minutes. Remove from the heat.

3. Meanwhile, bring a large pot of salted water to a boil over high heat. Add the mezze rigatoni and cook according to the package directions until it is al dente. Drain well, reserving ½ cup of the pasta cooking water.

4. Add the mezze rigatoni to the pan with the guanciale and toss to coat. Whisk ¼ cup of the pasta water into the reserved egg mixture to combine, then add it to the pan. Toss, adding pasta water a tablespoon at a time as needed, until a glossy sauce forms and coats the pasta.

5. Plate the mezze rigatoni and top each serving with one of the remaining egg yolks. Serve hot.

Note: If you are worried about consuming raw egg yolks, try using pasteurized eggs. They are a safe alternative available in most major supermarkets.

Serves 2

Toppings

Finely grated Parmigiano and pecorino

Freshly ground black pepper

Crushed red pepper flakes

A blend of milk and beef stock in béchamel, boosted with Worcestershire, does a great job of mimicking French onion soup, especially when you stir in caramelized onions. Take your time caramelizing the onions—the slow-cooked onions add incredible sweetness and depth. Cooking the onions low and slow tempers their sharpness and coaxes out their natural sugars, but if you're in a hurry and have a pressure cooker, you can do the onions at high pressure in about 20 minutes.

FRENCH ONION MAC AND CHEESE

Serves 4

Toppings

Crushed red pepper flakes
Fresh thyme

5x Better

Boost the flavor by topping the pasta with Crispy Garlic Breadcrumbs (page 113)

5 tablespoons unsalted butter

3 medium yellow onions, peeled and thinly sliced

Salt

8 ounces dried mezze rigatoni or macaroni

¼ cup all-purpose flour

1¼ cups whole milk

1¼ cups sodium-free beef stock

1 teaspoon Worcestershire sauce

1 tablespoon fresh thyme

½ teaspoon freshly ground black pepper

2 cups grated Gruyère cheese

1. Melt 2 tablespoons of the butter in a large sauté pan over medium heat. Add the onions, a handful at a time, tossing to coat with the butter. Season with a pinch of salt, then reduce the heat to medium-low and cook, stirring every 15 minutes, until the onions are deeply golden brown and caramelized, 45 minutes.

2. When the onions are just about done, bring a large pot of salted water to a boil over high heat. Add the rigatoni and cook according to the package directions until it is al dente. Drain well.

3. When the onions are done cooking, transfer them to a bowl and set aside. Melt the remaining 3 tablespoons butter in the sauté pan over medium heat. Whisk in the flour until smooth and completely incorporated, about 3 minutes. Whisk in the milk in a thin stream until the mixture smooths out into a thick paste, then whisk in the beef stock and Worcestershire. Let cook, stirring occasionally, until the sauce thickens, about 10 minutes.

4. Remove the sauce from the heat and add the thyme, ½ teaspoon of salt, the pepper, and the Gruyère. Stir until the cheese is melted, then stir in the caramelized onions and rigatoni to combine. Adjust the seasoning to taste. Serve hot.

 A large sauté pan is ideal for caramelizing onions—the high straight sides make it difficult for onions to jump out of the pan while you're stirring, and the large base helps the liquid evaporate so the onions caramelize instead of steaming.

This cozy mac and cheese is all about classic fall flavors: earthy pumpkin and crispy sage. Bonus: It's almost as fast to make as the boxed stuff. Cooking the pasta in milk, without draining it, emulsifies the pasta starch and sauce together, resulting in a smooth cheese sauce. The sauce starts out looking quite thin, but after you stir in the cheese and let it rest, it thickens up to the perfect consistency. It's an easy recipe to riff from—if you want a more traditional stovetop mac and cheese, leave out the pumpkin.

AUTUMN ALL YEAR

PUMPKIN SAGE MAC AND CHEESE

4 tablespoons (½ stick) unsalted butter

20 to 25 fresh whole sage leaves

3 tablespoons all-purpose flour

2 cups whole milk

1 teaspoon garlic powder

½ teaspoon dry mustard powder

½ teaspoon onion powder

8 ounces dried ziti or macaroni

2¼ cups grated Cheddar cheese

¾ cup canned pure pumpkin puree

Salt and freshly ground black pepper

1. Melt the butter in a large sauté pan or pot over medium heat. Add the sage leaves, being careful not to crowd the pan, and fry until crisp, 5 to 15 seconds, depending on the size of the leaves. Remove the crisp leaves to a paper towel to drain. Set aside.

2. Whisk the flour into the melted butter and cook, whisking constantly, until the flour is a blond color and the mixture is smooth, 1 to 2 minutes. Slowly whisk in 1 cup of the milk in a thin stream, continuing to whisk until any lumps are gone and the sauce is smooth and quite thick, 1 to 2 minutes.

3. Add the remaining 1 cup of milk along with 2½ cups of water, as well as the garlic, mustard, and onion powders. Add the uncooked ziti and stir until wisps of steam come up, 2 to 3 minutes. Reduce the heat to medium low. Let cook, gently bubbling, until the ziti is tender and the sauce starts to thicken, 9 to 10 minutes. (It will still be quite saucy at this point—adding the cheese will thicken it up.)

4. Remove the pan from the heat and stir in the cheese and pumpkin puree. Season to taste with salt and pepper and let stand for a couple of minutes; the sauce will thicken as it rests. Crumble the crispy sage leaves on top, and serve hot.

Serves 4

Toppings

Freshly grated nutmeg
Finely grated
   Parmigiano

Mentaiko, or karashi mentaiko, is Japanese spicy cod roe marinated in salt and red pepper flakes. It has a unique briny spicy-savory flavor slightly reminiscent of Italian bottarga (dried cured fish roe), and it pairs immensely well with the richness of mac and cheese. Along with a hint of funk from the kimchi, this mac and kimcheese is a classic Japanese combination with pockets of intense umami flavor.

MENTAIKO MAC

SPICY "CAVIAR" MAC AND KIMCHEESE

Serves 2

Toppings

Crispy Garlic
  Breadcrumbs
  (page 113)
Toasted sesame seeds
Sliced green onions

1 sac karashi mentaiko
  (see Note)

½ cup roughly chopped
  kimchi

Salt

6 ounces dried fusilli,
  bucati, or macaroni

1½ tablespoons unsalted
  butter

2 tablespoons all-
  purpose flour

1¼ cups whole milk

1¼ cups grated Cheddar
  cheese

Freshly ground black
  pepper

1. Cut open the mentaiko with a paring knife, then use a spoon to gently scoop out the insides (discard the membrane) and transfer to a small bowl. Stir in the kimchi and set aside.

2. Bring a large pot of salted water to a boil over high heat. Add the fusilli and cook according to the package directions until it is al dente. Drain well.

3. Meanwhile, melt the butter in a medium sauté pan over medium heat. Whisk in the flour and cook, whisking constantly, until the flour is a blond color and the mixture is smooth, 1 to 2 minutes. Slowly whisk in the milk in a thin stream, continuing to whisk until any lumps are gone. Let cook, stirring occasionally, until the sauce is smooth and quite thick, about 10 minutes.

4. Remove the sauce from the heat and add 1 cup of the Cheddar cheese. Stir until the cheese is just melted. Add the pasta and half of the mentaiko mixture, stirring to combine and coat the pasta evenly. Season with salt and pepper to taste.

5. Scoop the pasta into two bowls and top each with the remaining ¼ cup Cheddar cheese and the mentaiko mixture. Serve hot.

Note: You can find karashi mentaiko in the frozen section of most Japanese or Korean markets. Defrost it at room temperature before using (it should only take a few minutes).

Restaurant beef chow fun (we call it BCF) is made from fresh, flat, wide rice noodles special-ordered from rice noodle masters. You could go the same route and trek out to Chinatown for fresh noodles every time you want to make chow fun at home—or you can keep a package of dried noodles in the pantry and cook them whenever the craving hits. Dried rice noodles keep almost indefinitely and don't break up as much as fresh noodles when you're stir-frying.

AUTHENTIC BEEF CHOW FUN WITH 2 KINDS OF SOY SAUCE

Serves 4

Toppings

Sliced green onions
Toasted sesame seeds
Chili oil (preferably homemade; see page 53)

5 tablespoons light soy sauce

4 teaspoons Shaoxing wine (see page 235)

2 teaspoons toasted sesame oil

2 teaspoons cornstarch

2 cloves garlic, peeled and thinly sliced

1 pound rib-eye steak, thinly sliced

1 tablespoon dark soy sauce

1 teaspoon sugar

8 ounces dried wide rice noodles

2 tablespoons neutral oil

1 small red or white onion, peeled and sliced

2 cups mung bean sprouts

4 green onions, trimmed and sliced into matchsticks

1. Whisk together 1 tablespoon of the light soy sauce with 2 teaspoons of the Shaoxing wine and the sesame oil, cornstarch, and garlic in a large bowl. Add the beef and toss to coat. Marinate at room temperature for at least 15 minutes and up to 2 hours.

2. Make the sauce: Combine the remaining 4 tablespoons light soy sauce and 2 teaspoons Shaoxing wine with the dark soy sauce, sugar, and 1 tablespoon water in a small bowl. Stir well and set aside.

3. Bring a large pot of water to a boil over high heat. Add the noodles and cook according to the package directions. Drain the noodles, then rinse them in cold water and drain well again.

4. Heat a wok or large nonstick frying pan over high heat, then add the neutral oil. When the oil is hot, add the beef with its marinade and stir-fry until the meat is starting to brown, about 1 minute. Add the sliced red or white onion and continue to cook, stirring, until the beef is seared and brown, 2 to 3 minutes. Add the noodles to the pan and toss gently until the noodles are loose, then add the sauce. Sear, tossing and stirring, until everything is smoky and slightly charred, about 2 minutes.

5. Remove from the heat and stir in the bean sprouts and green onions. Serve hot.

One of the keys to this recipe is the dark soy sauce. We tested this with and without, and there's no contest. If you're a BCF fanatic, it's worth the extra bottle in your pantry.

Alla Gricia is the perfect combination of gloriously glossy bites of pasta coated in pecorino and black pepper with plenty of crispy guanciale. It's the pasta of Italian dreams. The key is starchy pasta water: After slowly rendering the fat out of your guanciale, you whisk it with a bit of the water over high heat to emulsify it into a sauce. Add the pecorino off the heat to avoid clumping, and finish with freshly cracked black pepper for just a touch of spice.

NEXT LEVEL ALLA GRICIA

GIANT PENNE WITH CRISPY GUANCIALE

Salt

4 ounces guanciale (see Tip, page 8), cut into ¾-inch strips

6 ounces dried penne giganti (aka giant penne)

2 teaspoons freshly cracked black pepper

2 ounces finely grated pecorino Romano cheese

1. Bring a large pot of salted water to a boil over high heat.

2. Meanwhile, cook the guanciale in a large sauté pan over medium heat until the fat renders and the guanciale is browned and crisp, 4 to 6 minutes. Use a slotted spoon to transfer the guanciale to a small bowl, leaving the rendered fat in the pan.

3. Add the penne giganti to the boiling water and cook according to the package directions until 3 minutes shy of al dente. Drain well, reserving 1½ cups of the pasta cooking water.

4. Add ¾ cup of the reserved pasta water to the fat in the pan and bring to a gentle boil over medium heat, swirling or whisking to emulsify, about 1 minute. Add the penne giganti to the pan and cook, tossing occasionally and adding pasta water ¼ cup at a time as needed, until the penne giganti is cooked al dente and the sauce becomes thick and glossy, about 3 minutes.

5. Remove from the heat and stir in the crispy guanciale and black pepper. Stir in the cheese until it's melted, thinning the sauce with extra pasta water if needed. Serve immediately.

Serves 2

Toppings

Freshly cracked black pepper
Finely grated pecorino Romano
Crushed red pepper flakes
Finely grated Parmigiano

We've done multiple tests on the best way to cook a meatball, and braising wins, hands down, every time. Slow braising gives you tender, flavorful meatballs that release their juices into the sauce, making it rich and even more savory. Bonus: Our giant meatballs are made from a combination of beef for savory meatiness, pork for fatty sweetness, and plenty of roasted garlic for a hit of mellow garlicky warmth. These very extra giant meatballs need a noodle that can hold up, and spaghettoni, with its extra thickness, is the answer.

SUPER SPAGHETTI AND MEATBALLS

SPAGHETTONI AND ROASTED GARLIC FENNEL MEATBALLS

1 head garlic, cloves separated and peeled

¼ cup olive oil

1 cup finely shredded carrot

1 cup finely chopped yellow onion

1 tablespoon fennel seeds, crushed

1 can (28 ounces) crushed tomatoes

3 cups cubed white bread, crusts removed

1 cup whole milk

½ pound ground beef

½ pound ground pork

2 large eggs

¾ cup finely grated Parmigiano-Reggiano cheese

2 tablespoons finely chopped fresh flat-leaf parsley

Salt and freshly ground black pepper

12 ounces dried spaghettoni

1. Preheat your oven to 375°F.

2. Lay a sheet of aluminum foil on a work surface, place the garlic cloves in the center, coat the garlic with 2 tablespoons of the oil, then wrap tightly in the foil. Roast the garlic in the oven until tender, 45 minutes, then remove from the oven and let cool completely in the foil.

3. Meanwhile, make the sauce: Heat the remaining 2 tablespoons of the oil in a large pot over medium heat. Add the carrot, onion, and 1 teaspoon of crushed fennel seeds. Cook until the vegetables are slightly soft but not brown, about 5 minutes, then stir in the tomatoes and 1 cup of water. Reduce the heat and hold at a simmer, covered, until needed (Step 6).

4. When the garlic is roasted, place the bread cubes in a large bowl, add the milk, and let soak until the bread is saturated, 1 to 2 minutes. Squeeze the bread with your hands to remove as much milk as possible; discard the milk. Return the bread to the bowl.

5. Using your hands, break up the bread into pea-size breadcrumbs. Mix in the ground meats, eggs, roasted garlic cloves, the remaining 2 teaspoons crushed fennel, the Parmigiano, parsley, ½ teaspoon salt, and ½ teaspoon black pepper until a homogenous, but loose, mixture forms.

Continued on next page ⟶

Serves 4

Toppings

Finely grated Parmigiano
Chopped fresh basil
Crushed red pepper flakes

5x Better

Boost the flavors by lightly toasting the fennel seeds in a dry pan over low heat before crushing them.

Make It Ahead

The meatballs and sauce can be made ahead of time and stored together in an airtight container in the fridge for up to 2 days. Cook your pasta according to the package directions, then reheat ½ cup of sauce (plus meatballs) per portion of pasta in a nonstick skillet and simmer the pasta in the pan for a minute or two. It will taste like you just slaved over a stove for hours.

6. Lightly wet your hands and form the mixture into large meatballs of about ¼ cup each, and drop them directly into the gently simmering sauce as you form them. Simmer, partially covered, until the meatballs are cooked through, 30 to 45 minutes. Flip the meatballs after about 15 minutes to ensure even cooking.

7. Bring a large pot of salted water to a boil over high heat. Add the spaghettoni and cook according to the package directions until 3 minutes shy of al dente. Drain well, reserving 1 cup of the pasta cooking water.

8. Use a slotted spoon to transfer the meatballs from the sauce to a large plate. Season the sauce to taste with salt and pepper, then add the drained spaghettoni to the sauce. If the sauce seems too thick, thin it with the reserved pasta water a tablespoon at a time. Cook until the pasta is al dente, 2 to 3 minutes.

9. Transfer the pasta to a platter and top with the meatballs. Serve hot.

Spaghettoni—literally "thick little twine"—is just a thicker version of regular spaghetti. If you can't find any, sub in your favorite thick pasta of choice, such as bucatini or linguine.

low STRESS TO DECOMPRESS

EASY WEEKNIGHT NOODLES

Easy recipes aren't second-class citizens.

Often they're just as delicious and satisfying as the crazy recipes that require eight hours and fifty ingredients to make. To us, the best recipes are the ones that people actually use. We love it when people tell us they made one of our recipes and it exceeded their expectations—and these are often the ones that are fast, uncomplicated, and low-effort. This chapter features the recipes we go to on weeknights, when we're too tired even to think about walking to the neighborhood pasta place or noodle joint.

Green onion oil is a beloved condiment and sauce in most of Asia. It adds a touch of fresh green umami to almost anything, especially noodles, and it's often so tasty it's the only flavor needed. If you want to make good green onion oil, you need to bring the heat. Hot oil is the key, mellowing and softening the raw bite of the green onions into a super savory aromatic sauce. Green onion oil goes well on just about anything, but noodles are the best vehicle. We like the purity of combining green onion oil and naked noodles, but feel free to add soy sauce, hoisin, or oyster sauce to mix it up.

TEENAGE MUTANT NINJA NOODLES

GREEN ONION OIL CHOW MEIN

1 cup thinly sliced green onions

½ cup neutral oil

Salt

12 ounces fresh chow mein noodles

1. Place the green onions in a large, deep, heatproof bowl.

2. Heat the oil in a pot over medium heat until it reaches 275°F on an instant-read thermometer, 1 to 2 minutes. (If you don't have an instant-read thermometer, place an uncoated wooden chopstick or spoon in the oil; if bubbles form around it, the oil is hot enough.)

3. Remove the pot from the heat and very carefully pour the hot oil over the green onions in the bowl—they will sizzle and the oil will bubble up. Once it is cool, taste and season with salt, then set aside.

4. Briefly cook the noodles according to the package directions. Drain well, then add the noodles to the green onion oil and toss until well coated. These noodles are equally good hot, room temp, or cold.

 If you're not in the mood for chow mein, any shape of pasta (cooked in salted water) will work beautifully with this oil as well.

Serves 4

Toppings

Chili oil (preferably homemade; see page 53)
Toasted sesame seeds
Thinly sliced Thai chili pepper

5x Better

Level up your green onion oil with gingery-garlicky flavor: Add 1 tablespoon each of finely minced peeled ginger, garlic, and shallot to the bowl with the green onions before adding the oil. Or, if you like it on the spicy side, add 1 to 2 sliced Thai chilies right after you combine the hot oil with the green onions

These are the most garlicky, buttery noodles you might ever have. There are two heads of garlic in these noodles, but its sharp bite is mellowed out in a gentle butter bath, giving the dish a robust garlic flavor that merges superbly with the sweet, briny umami of oyster sauce. Make sure you get a bottle of sauce that actually includes oysters as an ingredient—a good choice is the one from Lee Kum Kee. Look for the boat on the label.

SECRET INGREDIENT NOODLES

GARLIC-BUTTER BUCATINI WITH OYSTER SAUCE

Serves 4

Toppings

Crispy fried onions (see page 239)
Sliced green onions
Chopped fresh cilantro

Salt

12 ounces dried bucatini

6 tablespoons (¾ stick) unsalted butter

2 small heads garlic, cloves peeled and pressed or minced (see Tip)

3 tablespoons oyster sauce

2 teaspoons toasted sesame oil

Freshly ground black pepper

1. Bring a large pot of salted water to a boil over high heat. Add the bucatini and cook according to the package directions until it is 3 minutes shy of al dente. Drain well, reserving 1½ cups of the pasta cooking water.

2. Meanwhile, heat the butter and garlic in a sauté pan over very low heat. You don't want the garlic to brown; you're just looking to take the raw edge off and gently infuse the butter with flavor. Cook, stirring, until the butter smells amazingly garlicky, 4 to 5 minutes.

3. Turn the heat up to medium. Slowly whisk ¾ cup of the pasta water into the melted butter until the mixture is emulsified and gently boiling, about 2 minutes. Stir in the oyster sauce and sesame oil, then add the drained pasta. Cook, tossing occasionally, until the pasta is al dente and the sauce reduces and becomes thick and glossy, about 3 minutes. If the pasta starts to look dry, add more of the reserved pasta water ¼ cup at a time. Season with salt and pepper to taste, then serve immediately.

tip!

A good garlic press is your friend. If you have a heavy one, use it to smash the cloves before peeling the skin off, then press the garlic directly into the pan.

Black bean–beef chow mein is one of our favorite Chinese takeout dishes. The addictive combination of charred and smoky flash-fried beef, savory black bean sauce, and crispy chow mein noodles is very simple to make at home. The key ingredient, black bean sauce, is a specialty Chinese ingredient that you can find pretty easily in a large supermarket, in an Asian grocery store, or online.

A CHINESE DINER CLASSIC

RIB EYE WITH BLACK BEAN SAUCE AND CRISPY CHOW MEIN

2 tablespoons light soy sauce

2 tablespoons toasted sesame oil

¼ cup Shaoxing wine (see page 235)

¼ cup cornstarch

1 pound rib-eye steak, thinly sliced against the grain (see Tip)

6 cloves garlic, peeled and pressed or minced

2 tablespoons Chinese black bean sauce

2 tablespoons oyster sauce

Freshly ground black pepper

12 ounces chow mein noodles, preferably fresh

2 tablespoons neutral oil

1 medium yellow onion, peeled and sliced

2 green bell peppers, stemmed, seeded, and sliced

1. Whisk together the soy sauce, sesame oil, 2 tablespoons of the Shaoxing wine, and 2 tablespoons of the cornstarch in a medium bowl. Stir in the beef to coat thoroughly. Set aside to marinate.

2. Make the sauce: Stir together the garlic, black bean sauce, oyster sauce, the remaining 2 tablespoons each of Shaoxing wine and cornstarch, and 1½ teaspoons of black pepper (or to taste) in a small bowl. Set aside.

3. Cook the noodles according to the package directions. Drain well.

4. Heat a large wok or skillet over medium-high heat. When the pan is hot, add 1 tablespoon of the neutral oil and swirl to coat. When the oil starts to shimmer, about 1 minute, add the noodles and toss to distribute the oil evenly, then reduce the heat to low and cook, undisturbed, until the noodles are crisp, 2 to 3 minutes. Transfer the noodles to a platter.

5. Turn the heat up to medium-high and add the remaining 1 tablespoon of the neutral oil to the wok. Once the oil is hot, add the beef with its marinade and stir-fry until the meat is starting to brown, about 1 minute. Then add the onion, bell peppers, the reserved sauce, and 1 cup of water. Continue stir-frying until the sauce has reduced and is thick and glossy, 1 to 2 minutes.

6. Scoop the beef mixture over the crispy noodles and serve immediately.

Serves 4

Toppings

Chili oil (preferably homemade; see page 53)
Sliced green onions
Toasted sesame seeds

tip!

If you look closely at any steak, you'll see that the lines in the meat run in a parallel manner—this is the direction of the grain. Typically, but not always, butchers will cut the steak so that the grain runs along the long axis. Slicing against the grain means cutting perpendicular to the grain (or along the short axis, usually). This will produce a tender bite. For this dish, we like to slice our beef as thinly as possible.

Cold smashed cucumber salads are one of our summertime staples. The combo of refreshing chilled cucumbers and tangy sweet rice vinegar hits all the right notes. Working off the classic, we added pasta and thinly sliced fennel for extra texture and crunch. This is a great salad to serve alongside grilled meats; the vinegary dressing cuts through the richness of the meat and acts like a palate-cleansing counterpoint.

THE COLD AND THE CRISP

SMASHED CUCUMBER PASTA SALAD

Salt

12 ounces radiatore or other short pasta

⅔ cup rice vinegar

¼ cup neutral oil

2 tablespoons toasted sesame oil

2 tablespoons soy sauce

2 tablespoons sugar

4 cloves garlic, peeled and pressed or minced

Freshly ground black pepper

1 bulb fennel, trimmed and thinly sliced, fronds reserved

2 thin-skinned seedless cucumbers (such as English), smashed into chucks with a rolling pin or wine bottle

2 cups chopped fresh cilantro

1. Bring a large pot of salted water to a boil over high heat. Add the radiatore and cook according to the package directions until it is al dente. Drain well.

2. Meanwhile, whisk together the rice vinegar, oils, soy sauce, sugar, garlic, 1 teaspoon of salt, and ½ teaspoon of pepper to make a dressing.

3. Transfer the radiatore to a large bowl and add the fennel and fennel fronds, cucumbers, and cilantro. Add the dressing to taste and toss to mix. Season with salt and pepper to taste. Serve at room temperature or chilled.

Serves 4

Toppings

Toasted sesame seeds
Crispy fried onions
  (see page 239)
Chopped fresh cilantro

This salad keeps well in the fridge, so go ahead and whip up a batch for meal prep and enjoy it throughout the week. Hold off on the toppings, if using, until serving so they stay fresh and crisp.

When you're craving beef chow fun (aka BCF; see page 28) in the summer, but can't stand the idea of standing beside a hot wok, make this steak noodle salad instead. Bright and fresh with summer tomatoes and mint, this is the answer when you want a hands-off meal. Best of all, reverse searing will be the easiest way you've ever made steak. A low oven brings the steak up to a rosy medium-rare and a quick sear or grill gives it char.

LONG SUMMER NIGHTS

STEAK AND HEIRLOOM TOMATO NOODLE SALAD

Serves 4

5x Better

Toss in some sliced Thai chilies for heat and some crispy fried onions (see page 239) and toasted sesame seeds for crunch.

1 pound boneless rib eye steak

Salt and freshly ground black pepper

3 tablespoons neutral oil

1 clove garlic, peeled and pressed or minced

3 tablespoons rice vinegar

1 tablespoon toasted sesame oil

1 tablespoon fish sauce

1 tablespoon sugar

6 ounces dried wide rice noodles

4 or 5 small heirloom tomatoes, stemmed and sliced

5 or 6 radishes, trimmed and thinly sliced

½ English cucumber or 2 Persian cucumbers, trimmed and sliced

¼ cup roughly chopped fresh mint

1. Heat the oven to 200°F with a rack in the middle position.

2. Generously season the steak on both sides with salt and pepper, then place the steak on a wire rack set over a rimmed baking sheet. Transfer to the oven and cook until the internal temperature reaches 135°F, about 20 minutes (this will be medium-rare; adjust to your preference). Remove from the oven.

3. Heat 1 tablespoon of the neutral oil in a hot skillet or sauté pan over high heat. Add the steak and sear, turning once, until browned on both sides, 1 to 2 minutes per side. Transfer the steak to a cutting board and let rest for 5 to 10 minutes. Slice against the grain into ¼-inch slices. Set aside.

4. Whisk together the remaining 2 tablespoons of neutral oil with the garlic, rice vinegar, sesame oil, fish sauce, and sugar in a large bowl to make a dressing. Taste and adjust the seasoning if needed and set aside.

5. Cook the noodles according to the package directions. Drain, rinse in cold running water, then drain well.

6. Add the noodles, steak, tomatoes, radishes, cucumber, and mint to the dressing in the bowl and toss well to combine. Serve immediately.

Reverse searing—cooking steak in a low oven to bring the internal temperature of the steak to your desired doneness, then finishing it on the stove—is probably the easiest way to cook steak for a crowd. Since the oven is on, why not cook a couple extra?

There's something about a citrus-forward cold noodle salad that can cool you right down. Slippery chewy noodles, sweet shrimp, crunchy celery, and savory tomatoes all tossed in a sweet-tart fish sauce is better than air conditioning on a hot day.

Skinny Vermicelli

TOMATO LIME SHRIMP COLD NOODLE SALAD

2 cloves garlic, peeled and crushed

2 tablespoons sugar

1 Thai chili, stemmed and sliced (optional)

¼ cup fresh lime juice

2 tablespoons fish sauce

4 bundles (3 ounces each) rice vermicelli threads

1 pound large shrimp, peeled and deveined

2 or 3 ribs celery, cut diagonally into 2-inch strips (see Note)

1 pint mini heirloom cherry tomatoes, halved

½ cup roughly chopped fresh cilantro

2 or 3 green onions, thinly sliced

1. Make the dressing: Using a mortar and pestle, crush the garlic, sugar, and Thai chili, if using, into a paste (alternatively, finely mince the garlic and chili into a fine paste, then add the sugar). Transfer to a small bowl and stir in the lime juice, fish sauce, and ½ cup of water. Set aside.

2. Cook the vermicelli according to the package directions. Drain, rinse in cold running water, then drain well.

3. Bring a medium pot of water to a boil over high heat. Prepare a bowl of ice water. Boil the shrimp until plump, pink, and firm, 2 to 3 minutes, then use a slotted spoon to immediately transfer them to the ice water bath. Once cool, drain well.

4. Place the noodles in a large serving bowl and add the shrimp, celery, cherry tomatoes, cilantro, and green onions. Drizzle with the dressing to taste and toss to combine, then serve immediately.

Note: Celery leaves are deliciously delicate and complex. If your celery comes with the leaves attached, you should totally add them to the salad in Step 4.

Serves 4

5x Better

Top the salad with crispy fried onions (see page 239) and thinly sliced raw shallots for a dynamic double crunch.

Feel free to halve the lime juice if you prefer a less intense flavor (you can always add more to taste).

THIS ESSENTIAL HOMEMADE

CHILI OIL

IS WHAT YOU NEED IN YOUR FRIDGE

The Essential Chili Oil is deliciously fragrant, dark ruby red, spicy but not too spicy, with a complex smoky toasted background and a hint of classic Chinese aromatics. It keeps well in the fridge and is good on virtually everything: meats, seafood, eggs, rice, and especially noodles.

The key is to infuse the oil in two steps, first heating it with aromatics on the stove, then pouring it over chili flakes, which makes them bubble up, release their spicy aroma, and get a little crisp. Cooking the chili flakes this way ensures that you don't burn them and end up with bitter oil.

Chinese chili flakes are the way to go with this recipe. They're more vibrant and contain fewer seeds than the standard Italian-style crushed red pepper flakes you'll find at most grocery stores. They add a crunchy crisp element to the oil. You can buy Chinese chili flakes at an Asian grocery store or online. (If you're not in the mood to make your own chili oil, you can also buy it prepared in jars. Every brand is different, so if you go the premade route, make sure to taste it so that you know you like the flavor and spice level before using it in a recipe.)

Go on, make a double batch—you know you want to!

THE ESSENTIAL
Chili Oil

¼ cup Chinese chili flakes (see page 239)

⅔ cup neutral oil

1-inch piece fresh ginger, peeled and sliced

2 bay leaves

2 star anise pods

1 cinnamon stick

3 green onions, white parts only

2 teaspoons whole Sichuan peppercorns (see Tip)

Salt

1. Place 2 tablespoons of the chili flakes in a medium heatproof bowl. Set aside.

2. Combine the oil, ginger, bay leaves, star anise, cinnamon stick, green onions, and peppercorns in a small saucepan over medium-low heat. Heat until the mixture bubbles gently and the green onions start to brown (or until the oil reaches 300°F on an instant-read thermometer), 5 to 6 minutes. Let steep for another 10 minutes, never letting the temperature go over 300°F. Remove from the heat and use a slotted spoon to remove the solids from the infused oil in the pot.

3. Return the oil in the pot to medium heat and cook until it is hot and shimmering (it will read 350°F on an instant-read thermometer), 1 to 2 minutes. Carefully pour the infused hot oil into the bowl with the chili flakes—they will sizzle and bubble up. Let rest for 5 minutes, then mix in the remaining chili flakes. The oil should be bright red.

4. Let cool, then taste and season with salt. The chili oil will keep in a clean sealed jar in the fridge for up to 2 weeks.

Makes about ½ cup

tip!

You can easily buy whole Sichuan peppercorns at an Asian grocery store or online.

We like to make a big batch of these noodles for a night of staying in, eating noodles, and binge-watching whole TV series. These aren't your standard takeout sesame peanut noodles. First off, there's no peanut butter—instead, deep and distinctively nutty sesame paste and chili oil contribute the bulk of the texture and flavor. A hint of Chinese black vinegar, with its malty, slightly sweet bite, cuts the richness of the sesame paste and plays off the heat of the chili oil. Balanced and complex, these noodles hit all the right flavor notes.

LET'S STAY IN TONIGHT!

SPICY SESAME CHILI OIL NOODLES

12 ounces fresh or 6 ounces dried noodles (see Notes)

2 tablespoons light soy sauce

2 tablespoons Chinese sesame paste (see Notes)

1½ tablespoons chili oil (preferably homemade; see page 53)

1 tablespoon toasted sesame oil

2 teaspoons Chinese black vinegar (see Notes)

1. Cook the noodles according to the package directions. Drain well, reserving ¼ cup of the noodle cooking water.

2. Meanwhile, whisk together the soy sauce, sesame paste, chili oil, sesame oil, and black vinegar in a large bowl.

3. Add the noodles to the sauce, tossing to coat them well. Loosen the sauce with noodle water if needed. Serve immediately.

Notes: This recipe calls for your favorite noodle of choice. We prefer Shangxi planed noodles (pictured), which are ruffle-edged dried Chinese knife-cut noodles, easily found at any Asian grocery store, but you can use any noodle you like or have on hand—you are staying in tonight, after all! As a rough guide, go for 4 to 6 ounces of fresh noodles or 3 ounces of dried noodles per person.

If you can't find Chinese sesame paste, try substituting tahini or, in a pinch, sugar-free natural peanut butter.

Chinese black vinegar (see page 235) can be switched out for balsamic or any other vinegar you might have on hand.

Serves 2

Toppings

Sliced green onions
Crispy fried onions (see page 239)
Chopped fresh cilantro
Toasted sesame seeds

tip!

Don't like your sesame noodles spicy? Substitute hoisin sauce for the chili oil.

There are a multitude of Vietnamese bun (vermicelli) bowls that you can make at home, but the one that we turn to again and again—both for taste and ease—is this one: lemongrass-marinated char-grilled beef or chicken, thin rice noodles, and fresh herbs, all doused in a sweet-tart fish sauce vinaigrette. Pro tip: Make the vinaigrette the day before to let the flavors meld.

THE WEEKNIGHT BUN BOWL

LEMONGRASS BEEF VERMICELLI BOWL

Serves 4

Toppings

Crispy fried onions
    (see page 239)
Torn fresh herbs (mint,
    Thai basil, cilantro,
    and/or shiso)
Thinly sliced cabbage
Thinly sliced red onions

Variation

Feel free to swap out the beef for the meat of your choice. We often use boneless chicken thighs (as shown in the top bowl in the photo on the right).

If you hate mincing lemongrass try this: Remove the outer layer of the stalk, then use a Microplane grater to make fine shavings of the softer white parts.

2 stalks lemongrass, white parts only, minced

1 shallot, peeled and minced

4 cloves garlic, peeled and pressed or minced, plus 1 clove, peeled

¼ cup fish sauce

2 tablespoons sugar

1 pound thinly sliced flank or tri-tip steak

1 Thai chili, stemmed and sliced

Juice of ½ lime

12 ounces thin rice vermicelli noodles

1 small head lettuce, trimmed and torn into bite-size pieces

½ English cucumber or 2 Persian cucumbers, trimmed and thinly sliced crosswise

1 tablespoon neutral oil

1. Combine the lemongrass, shallot, 4 pressed garlic cloves, 2 tablespoons of fish sauce, and 1 tablespoon of sugar in a large ziplock bag. Add the steak, seal the bag, and turn to coat. Let marinate at room temperature while you complete the other steps.

2. Using a mortar and pestle, crush together the 1 peeled garlic clove, the Thai chili, and the remaining 1 tablespoon of sugar (alternatively, finely mince the garlic and chili into a fine paste, then add the sugar). Transfer to a small bowl and stir in 1 cup of water, the remaining 2 tablespoons of fish sauce, and the lime juice to make a vinaigrette. Set aside.

3. Meanwhile, cook the noodles according to the package directions. Rinse in cold water and drain well.

4. Divide the lettuce and cucumbers among four large bowls. Push the greens to one side and nestle an equal amount of vermicelli into each bowl.

5. Heat the oil in a large skillet over medium heat. When it is hot, add the beef and marinade, and stir-fry until crispy and cooked through, 6 to 10 minutes. Remove from the pan and divide it among the bun bowls. Serve with the fish sauce vinaigrette alongside for pouring over at the table.

Instant noodles are one of the greatest inventions of all time. A bold statement for sure, but more than 100 billion packages of instant noodles are eaten yearly, making Momofuku Ando's invention one of the most influential foods of our day and age. From their humble origins as a subsistence food, instant noodles have taken on a life of their own, becoming beloved and celebrated—even inspiring an instant noodle museum in Yokohama, Japan. With such widespread reach, instant noodles might be the one dish that each and every one of us has eaten regardless of where we're from. In a way, we're all at a common table, living that noodle life together.

One Noodle to Rule Them All

Instant noodles have the magical ability to transport you to places very far away. For those times when you want authentic noodles but are nowhere near a noodle shop, the right instant noodles can save the day—many come with flavor packs that taste surprisingly close to the real deal. Here are some brands that we love; they do an amazing job of approximating the dishes they claim to be.

Nongshim Shin Black Ramyun is a cult classic: thick and chewy noodles in a spicy beef soup. This Korean brand makes noodles so good that many Koreans prefer them to restaurant-made noodles. There are even shops dedicated to serving Nongshim noodles, swapping in their own creations for the soup bases and toppings.

Indomie Mi Goreng has the same kind of fan following and dedicated restaurants—people can't get enough of that sweet and slightly spicy fried noodle. Unlike most instant noodles, this one is not served in a soup but instead is drained and then tossed in a sauce that mimics classic Indonesian fried noodles.

Mama Shrimp Creamy Tom Yum, from the Thai brand Mama, does a fantastic (and trendy, though nontraditional) take on this popular dish: thin, curly noodles in a surprisingly spicy coconut soup.

Nissin's restaurant series carefully formulates recipes by actual chefs of famous ramen shops in Japan. The two most famous are the Michelin-starred ramen joints Nakiryu and Konjiki Hototogisu, but they've also done a collaboration with Ippudo that is especially on point.

We make it a point to go and check out the instant noodle aisles in every new city we visit, especially in Japan. The literal birthplace of instant noodles is home to so many fun varieties—we may or may not have come home with an entire suitcase filled with instant noodles on more than one occasion.

A note on instant noods: In most of our recipes, instant noodles can easily be used in place of egg or wheat noodles. Dry instant noodles are the way to go here; they're perfectly engineered to come out right every time. When you're using the noodles as an ingredient (sans flavor packet), it's best to go with a thicker variety—our favorite is Nongshim.

Soup Up Your Noods

Instant noodles are an amazing dish in and of themselves, and beloved by noodle lovers of all ages. Even the simplest package of humble instant noodles can be elevated with just a few key components. The next time you're craving a midnight noodle snack, live that noodle life with these ultimate upgrades.

The Ramen Egg: Top with a soy-marinated jammy ramen egg (page 217) or crispy fried egg, or simply stir an egg into the stock while the noodles are cooking. Top with sliced green onions and crispy fried onions (see page 239.)

Southeast Asian Inspired: Squeeze in lime juice and top with sliced red onions, sliced jalapeño, and fresh cilantro—good with any soupy instant noodle, but best with the spicy variety.

Instant Noodle Alfredo: Toss drained noodles with butter, then top with freshly shaved or grated Parmigiano-Reggiano and freshly cracked black pepper.

Protein Overload: Cut up Spam, hot dogs, deli meat, crispy bacon, cooked sausage, shrimp, tofu . . . anything your heart desires.

Classic Japanese: Drizzle on a bit of toasted sesame oil, then top with sliced green onions, nori, and toasted sesame seeds. **5**

Instant Noodle Salad: Add tofu and veggies like corn, cabbage, scallions, broccoli. Anything goes! **6**

Asian Carbonara: Drain the noodles and toss with 1 egg, 1 tablespoon oyster sauce, and a pinch of white pepper for a quick Asian take on carbonara. **7**

Spicy AF: Add gochujang, curry powder, harissa, za'atar, chili oil (see page 53), or chili flakes. **8**

Lazy XO Noodles: Drain the noodles and toss them with XO Sauce (page 225), fresh cilantro, and crispy fried onions (see page 239). **9**

63

We love Philly cheesesteaks, and we love noodles. One drunken night at home, we were talking about noodles and thought that mazemen ramen—a "dry" (soupless) style popular in Japan—could be the perfect base for the Philly cheesesteak. So of course we made it immediately with whatever we had on hand, which naturally meant instant noodles. For this dish, we season the instant noodle base with soy and oyster sauces and pair it with well-seared steak, green peppers, red onion, and Cheez Whiz. It's hotly contested whether cheesesteaks should be topped with Cheez Whiz or provolone, but in this case the Whiz wins hands down—it melts into the noodles perfectly.

PHILLY CHEESE NOODLES

PHILLY CHEESESTEAK INSTANT MAZEMEN

¼ pound thinly sliced rib eye, sirloin, or tri-tip steak

Salt and freshly ground black pepper

1 tablespoon neutral oil

½ green bell pepper, stemmed, seeded, and sliced

¼ red onion, peeled and sliced

1 package (4.2 ounces) Nongshim Shin Black Ramyun (see page 60), flavor packet omitted

2 tablespoons Cheez Whiz, or to taste

½ tablespoon soy sauce

½ tablespoon oyster sauce

1. Bring a small pot of water to a boil over high heat. Season the steak on both sides with salt and pepper.

2. Meanwhile, heat the oil in a large nonstick skillet or frying pan over medium-high heat. Add the bell pepper and onion and cook until slightly soft, 1 to 2 minutes, then move to the side of the pan and add the thinly sliced steak in a pile. Press down and sear until a crust forms on the bottom of the steak, about 2 minutes, then flip and sear the other side. Once a crust has formed on the other side, stir together the steak, bell pepper, and onion and cook until the steak is cooked through, another 2 minutes. Remove the pan from the heat and set aside.

3. Cook the instant noodles in the boiling water according to the package directions. Drain well. Return the noodles to the pot and stir in the Cheez Whiz, soy sauce, and oyster sauce until the noodles are coated evenly.

4. Transfer the noodles to a serving bowl, top with the steak mixture, and serve hot.

Serves 1

Toppings

Sliced green onions
Crispy fried shallots (see page 239)
Freshly cracked black pepper

Mazemen is a type of ramen that is popular in Japan but hasn't quite caught on in America. It's the perfect choice for people who don't grow up as expert high-speed noodle slurpers. The flavoring is placed under the noodles, which are cooked to perfection. When you get the bowl, you can customize it to your liking with extra flavorings and spicy oils, then toss to mix it all up. You can eat mazemen as slowly as you'd like, comfortable in the knowledge that your noodles will never become soggy (and therefore ruined). Two of our favorite mazemen spots in Tokyo are Gachi Oil Soba by Mensho, and Tokyo Abura Soba, a chain with a distinctive gray facade and red neon kanji sign that you can find all across Tokyo.

When we're tired and hankering for a quick, satisfyingly easy and tasty pasta, this is the formula we follow: noodles + fatty meat + aromatics + hearty greens. One of our favorites, time and again, is this version. The meat is Italian sausage, which renders out flavorful fat that emulsifies with the starchy pasta water and the liquid from the veg to yield a quick pan sauce. The hearty green is kale; it adds a contrasting note and makes us feel better about digging into a giant bowl of pasta. For the noodle, we use calamarata, a wide, circular pasta that looks, unsurprisingly, like calamari rings.

WEEKNIGHT PASTA TOSS

SAUSAGE, KALE, AND CALAMARATA

Salt

12 ounces dried calamarata or other short pasta

1 tablespoon neutral oil

4 Italian sausages (about 1 pound), casings removed

1 bunch kale, stemmed and torn into 2- to 3-inch pieces

1 leek, trimmed and rinsed, white and light green parts thinly sliced crosswise

½ shallot, peeled and sliced

1 serrano or other fresh chile, stemmed, seeded, and thinly sliced (optional)

½ cup finely grated Parmigiano-Reggiano cheese

Freshly ground black pepper

1. Bring a large pot of salted water to a boil over high heat. Cook the calamarata according to the package directions until it is 3 minutes shy of al dente. Drain, reserving 1½ cups of the pasta cooking water.

2. Heat the oil in a large sauté pan over medium-high heat. Remove the sausage meat from the casings and add it to the pan. Cook, breaking up the meat and stirring with a wooden spoon, until it is golden brown all over and crispy in spots, 5 to 8 minutes.

3. Add the kale, leek, shallot, and serrano, if using, to the pan and cook, stirring, until soft, 2 to 3 minutes. Add ½ cup of the reserved pasta water, stirring and scraping the bottom of the pan to release any browned bits, then bring to a gentle boil over medium heat, swirling or whisking to emulsify the water and fat, about 1 minute.

4. Add the calamarata to the pan and cook, tossing occasionally, until it is al dente and the sauce becomes thick and glossy, about 3 minutes.

5. Remove the pan from the heat. Add the cheese and stir until melted. Loosen the sauce with more pasta water, if needed, and season with salt and pepper to taste. Serve hot.

Serves 4

Toppings

Finely grated Parmigiano
Crushed red pepper flakes
Crispy Garlic Breadcrumbs (page 113)

5x Better

In Step 3, replace the pasta water with ½ cup of dry white wine, then simmer the sauce to reduce it by half for a more complex flavor.

3

PLEASE SEND NOODS

DISHES FOR DATE NIGHT AND OTHER FANCY TIMES

Forget about Netflix and chill—it's time to Netflix and noodle.

Do you really want to go out for another questionable meal where you have to dress up and pay extra for drinks? Forget about it. The best kind of date always ends in satisfaction. You know, the kind of satisfaction you get after making and eating a delicious meal. These are the special noodle recipes to pull out when you want to impress—whether you're cooking for a date or a friend or two. These dishes are so good that you'll want to have date night in all the time—even if it's just you (after all, once you taste these noodles, you may not want to share!).

Say "I love you" with lobster pasta. Homemade Spaghetti alla Chitarra and lobster in a white wine sauce might be the ultimate date night dinner. This lobster pasta has a double hit of lobster flavor from sweet lobster meat and pasta cooked in your own lobster stock. Using the discarded lobster shells to make a quick stock isn't anything new, but cooking your pasta in said water ramps the lobster flavor up to a whole other level. If you don't have the time or energy to make homemade spaghetti, you can sub any other long pasta, such as bucatini.

THE DOUBLE LOBSTER

CACIO E PEPE LOBSTER CHITARRA

Salt

4 lobster tails (6 to 8 ounces each)

2 portions (12 to 16 ounces) Spaghetti alla Chitarra (page 13) or 12 to 16 ounces fresh pasta of your choice

2 tablespoons (¼ stick) unsalted butter

4 cloves garlic, peeled and sliced

⅓ cup dry white wine

½ cup finely grated Parmigiano-Reggiano cheese

1 teaspoon freshly ground black pepper

1. In a pot large enough to hold all the lobster tails plus water, bring 4 cups of water plus a pinch of salt to a boil over high heat. Reduce the heat to medium and add the lobster tails. Poach at a simmer, uncovered, until just cooked through, about 8 minutes. While the lobster cooks, prepare a large bowl of ice water.

2. Using tongs, transfer the cooked lobster tails to the ice bath (reserve the cooking liquid, covered, over low heat). When they are cool enough to handle, pull the meat from the shells, roughly chop it, and set it aside. Return the shells to the cooking liquid in the pot and simmer to make a quick stock, 10 to 15 minutes.

3. Remove the shells with a slotted spoon and discard. Turn the heat up to high, and bring the stock to a boil. Add the pasta and cook until it just starts to float, 2 to 3 minutes. Drain well, reserving 1½ cups of the stock.

4. Meanwhile, melt the butter in a sauté pan over low heat. Add the garlic and cook, stirring, until it is fragrant and slightly golden, 4 to 5 minutes. Turn the heat up to medium and add the wine. Simmer until it is reduced by half, about 1 minute, then add ¼ cup of the stock to the pan—it may bubble up a bit—and bring it to a gentle boil, whisking or swirling often to emulsify.

5. Add the pasta and lobster meat to the sauce in the pan and cook, tossing occasionally, until the pasta is al dente and the sauce reduces and becomes thick and glossy, about 3 minutes.

6. Remove the pan from the heat and stir in the cheese until it melts, thinning out the sauce with extra stock if needed. Season with the pepper and salt to taste, and serve hot.

Serves 2

Toppings

Freshly grated lemon zest
Finely grated Parmigiano
Crispy Garlic Breadcrumbs (page 113)
Crushed red pepper flakes

This is sort of an easy lighter version of chef Michael White's inspired signature dish of bone marrow, red wine, and octopus. But the real inspiration for this dish is one beautifully lazy summer we spent in Málaga, Spain, years ago. We went to the market each day and bought fresh squid caught earlier that morning, cleaned for us by a friendly fishmonger who always asked if we wanted to keep the ink sac (the answer was no but should have been yes). It was a blissful, squid-filled summer of homemade calamari, squid paella, and, of course, squid pasta. Anytime we want to remember those balmy, carefree summer days, we make this pasta. It tastes like you have all the time in the world to sit back and watch life go by.

SURF 'N TURF

BONE MARROW AND SQUID MAFALDA

Serves 4

Toppings

Finely grated
  Parmigiano
Crushed red pepper
  flakes

2 beef marrow bones
  (about 2 inches long)

2 tablespoons olive oil

4 ounces guanciale,
  chopped

1 pound squid rings
  (see Tip)

1 clove garlic, peeled and
  sliced

2 tablespoons chopped
  carrot

½ small yellow onion,
  peeled and chopped

½ cup dry white wine

2 cups sodium-free
  chicken stock

Salt

12 ounces dried mafalda

¼ cup finely grated
  Parmigiano-Reggiano
  cheese

Freshly ground black
  pepper

1. Place the marrow bones in a small bowl and add warm water to cover. Let soak.

2. Combine the oil, guanciale, squid, and garlic in a large pot over medium-high heat and cook until the garlic just becomes fragrant, 1 minute. Add the carrot and onion and cook, stirring occasionally, until the onion is translucent and soft, about 5 minutes. Add the wine and simmer until it is reduced by half, 2 to 3 minutes. Add the chicken stock, reduce the heat to low, and cover. Simmer until the squid is fork-tender, about 30 minutes.

3. Bring a large pot of salted water to a boil over high heat. Add the mafalda and cook according to the package directions until it is 3 minutes shy of al dente. Drain well, reserving 1½ cups of the pasta cooking water.

4. Using your fingers, push on the marrow to pop it out of the bones. Chop it roughly and add it to the squid sauce, whisking until it has melted and the sauce is emulsified, 2 to 3 minutes.

5. Add the mafalda to the sauce in the pot along with the cheese and cook over medium heat, tossing gently, until the mafalda is al dente and the sauce is smooth and glossy, about 3 minutes. If the sauce seems too thick, add the reserved pasta water a tablespoon at a time to thin it. Season to taste with salt and pepper. Serve hot.

Frozen squid works just as well as fresh in this dish. If you opt for frozen, make life easier by going for the rings rather than the body or tentacles. There's no need to thaw it before using.

HELLO
my name is

Bun Bo Hue

Bun bo hue is one of the most famous dishes in Vietnam, and one of the very few to be so closely associated with a city (and its surrounding area). In fact, the name literally means "beef noodle soup from the city of Hue." It's been a classic street food for as long as anyone can remember, and there's no absolute right way to make it. In its lifetime, it's gone from a soup made only with beef to a beef-based soup with lots of other ingredients added in, such as pig's trotters and coagulated pork blood (similar to Scottish black pudding). Don't believe anyone who tells you what it needs to be authentic, though—the first bun bo hue had only slices of beef and rice noodles. Everything since has been a modern addition.

The key elements to a great bun bo hue are the spicy aromatic sate sauce made of lemongrass, shallots, garlic, and chilies; a gorgeous lemongrass-scented beef broth (it's not a pho broth, though some restaurants will try to pass off pho as the base); and thick, round rice noodles. Our version is simplified but still skirts the edge of being challenging and painstaking—it's a weekend project for sure, but totally worth it. If you can find fresh banana blossoms to top it, it'll be that much closer to something you'd get on the streets of Hue.

Great noodle soups go the distance when it comes to toppings. Here's everything we put on our BBH.

1 Vermicelli

Bun bo hue uses an extra-thick round rice vermicelli. You can usually find these dried in most larger grocery stores or specialty Asian grocery stores. In a pinch, try gluten-free spaghetti. The thickness of the vermicelli means a longer-than-usual cooking time, so you'll need to plan accordingly.

2 Flank Steak and Other Meats

We stew a tough cut of flank or brisket in the lemongrass beef broth until it becomes deliciously melt-in-your-mouth. Like pho, bun bo hue benefits from the tastes and textures of different cuts of meat, so feel free to use our guide to pho meats (see page 138) and add as many cuts as is practical.

3 Meatballs

Vietnamese meatballs are super dense and chewy in the best way. Because this is bun bo hue, you'll want to use beef meatballs. You can usually find them at an Asian supermarket. To prepare, slice in half and drop into boiling water or soup for a minute to heat up, and enjoy.

4 Meatloaf (Cha Chien)

There are dozens of kinds of Vietnamese meatloaf, but they all share a super-smooth homogenous texture and a delicious peppery porky flavor. The one we like best is called cha chien, which is the fried version. You can usually find it near the tofu and fresh noodles at an Asian grocery store.

5 Spicy Aromatic Sate

It's traditional to have extra sate at the table in case anyone wants more heat. If you like your food with extra kick, make double (or more) the amount of sate called for in the recipe and set some aside for the table. We make ours in bulk and keep it in the fridge to add to anything that needs a flavor and spice boost.

6 Banana Blossoms

The most authentic bun bo hue shops will usually top your soup with banana blossoms, which add crunch and a tangy complexity. This ingredient can be hard to find and even harder to prepare if you find whole blossoms instead of the prewashed, presliced stuff. If you can't find them, feel free to omit them.

7 Fresh Herbs

It wouldn't be a Vietnamese soup bowl without fresh herbs on top. For bun bo hue we use mint, cilantro, shiso, Vietnamese coriander (rau ram), and sawtooth coriander (ngo gai), plus thinly sliced red onion and mung bean sprouts.

8 Lime, Jalapeño, and Sprouts

Quarters of lime are always welcome to offset the rich spiciness of the broth. Sliced jalapeño adds a fresh bright hit of heat. Mung bean sprouts are offered blanched or raw—we prefer raw.

Pho (see page 137) is good, but bun bo hue is the noodle soup you never knew you loved: spicy, sweet, tangy, and meat heavy. You don't have to get every meat we recommend on page 78, but if you live near an Asian market, pick up whatever they have and you won't be disappointed. Vietnamese people elevate meatball (and meatloaf) making to a fine art. The fried meatloaf (cha chien) is especially good and might be one of the last poorly kept secrets in the food world.

Bun Bo Hue

THE NOODLE SOUP YOU NEVER KNEW YOU LOVED

2 quarts sodium-free beef stock

1 pound brisket, trimmed

2 shallots, peeled and halved

8 stalks lemongrass, trimmed

4 cloves garlic, peeled and pressed or minced

4 Thai chilies, stemmed (see Tip)

½ cup neutral oil

¼ cup sugar

¼ cup Chinese chili flakes

¼ cup fish sauce, plus extra for serving

12 ounces extra-thick rice vermicelli (see Note)

8 ounces Vietnamese meatloaf (about ½ loaf), sliced (optional)

8 Vietnamese beef meatballs, halved (optional)

Mung bean sprouts, lime wedges, sliced jalapeño, and fresh herbs, for serving

To cut the heat, leave out the Thai chilies or use fewer.

1. Combine the beef stock, brisket, and 2 of the shallot halves in a large saucepan or stockpot. Bend 4 stalks of the lemongrass so that they fit in the pot and add them, too. Bring to a boil over high heat, then reduce the heat to low and let simmer for 2 hours while you move on to the next steps.

2. Meanwhile, make the spicy aromatic sate: Mince the remaining lemongrass and transfer it to a food processor along with the remaining shallot, the garlic, and the Thai chilies. Pulse into a fine paste.

3. Heat the oil in a medium saucepan over medium-high heat until it shimmers. Add the sate paste and fry, stirring, just until fragrant, 1 to 2 minutes. Remove from the heat and add the sugar, chili flakes, and fish sauce. Stir to combine, then set the sate aside.

4. Thirty minutes before your broth is done or before you are ready to serve, bring a large pot of water to a boil over high heat. Add the vermicelli and cook it according to the package directions, then rinse with cold water and drain well.

5. Remove the brisket from the broth and allow it to rest on a cutting board or plate. Once it is cool enough to handle, slice the brisket into ¼-inch-thick slices. If you have meatloaf and meatballs, add them to the broth to warm through, 1 minute.

6. Assemble the soup bowls: Spoon 1 to 2 tablespoons of the sate into each of four warmed bowls. Top each with one-quarter of the vermicelli, 4 or 5 slices of brisket, and some meatloaf and meatballs, if using, then add 2 cups of the broth. Taste and adjust the seasoning with more sate or fish sauce. Serve hot, with bean sprouts, lime wedges, jalapeño, and herbs alongside.

Serves 4

Make It Ahead

You can make the broth, brisket, and sate in advance and store them in the fridge for up to 2 days. Wrap and store the brisket separately from the broth (chilling it allows it to slice even more cleanly than if you sliced it fresh from the broth). Reheat the sliced brisket in the broth before building your bowls.

5x Better

Make a double batch of the spicy aromatic sate made in Step 3 and save the extra for the table. If you can find banana blossoms (see page 78), throw some on top of the soup before serving.

Note: If you're shopping in a well-stocked Asian grocery store, look for the vermicelli labeled bun bo hue. Unlike most noodles, bun bo hue noodles can take up to 25 minutes to cook (follow the directions on the package, if any), so plan accordingly.

In Japan, if you're lucky and it's the right season, your miso soup will come with tiny clams. The brininess of the clams pairs perfectly with the sweet umami of miso, something we re-created here with this miso clam linguine. Steaming fresh clams with garlic, miso, and wine means that when the clams release their juice, everything combines into a quick clam broth that is perfect for tossing with pasta.

A CLAM WITH A PLAN

MISO CLAM LINGUINE

Serves 4

Toppings

Crispy Garlic
  Breadcrumbs
  (page 113)
Crushed red pepper
  flakes
Finely grated
  Parmigiano
Finely chopped fresh
  parsley

When buying fresh clams, give each one a tap. If the shell closes, it's alive. Leave the bag of clams open on the way home so they don't suffocate. Once you're home, store them in an open bowl, on ice, in the fridge.

Salt

4 tablespoons (½ stick)
  unsalted butter

8 cloves garlic, peeled
  and sliced

2 tablespoons white miso

½ cup dry white wine

2 pounds littleneck
  or Manila clams,
  scrubbed

12 ounces dried or
  24 ounces fresh
  linguine or other
  long pasta

¼ cup finely chopped
  fresh flat-leaf parsley

Freshly ground black
  pepper

1. Bring a large pot of salted water to a boil over high heat.

2. Meanwhile, make the sauce: Melt the butter in a large pot with a lid over medium heat, then add the garlic. When the garlic is soft, 2 to 3 minutes, whisk in the miso until smooth. Add the wine, bring to a boil, and cook until the wine has reduced by half, 3 to 5 minutes. Add the clams and cover the pot. Steam the clams until they open, lightly shaking the pan occasionally to ensure even cooking, 5 to 7 minutes. Open the pan and discard any clams that did not open. Use a slotted spoon to transfer the remaining clams to a medium bowl. Cover the bowl with aluminum foil.

3. Add the linguine to the boiling water and cook according to the package directions until it is 3 minutes shy of al dente. Drain well, reserving 1½ cups of the pasta cooking water.

4. Add ¾ cup of the reserved pasta water to the sauce in the pot and whisk until it is emulsified. Add the linguine and cook, tossing gently, until the linguine is al dente and the sauce is thick and glossy, about 3 minutes. Add pasta water as needed to thin the sauce.

5. Remove the pot from the heat and add the parsley, half of the clams, and any juices that have collected in the bowl. Toss to combine. Season with salt and pepper to taste. Serve the linguine topped with the remaining clams.

HELLO
my name is

NOODLE BOWL

"You know me—I'm that bowl you buy every week, sometimes even two times a week, down the street from the office? I'm healthy, I taste great, and you spend way too much money on me. You can't quit me and why would you want to? I look good and taste even better."

Yup, we're all guilty of it—buying an overpriced noodle bowl because we didn't do any planning at the beginning of the week. Noodle prep your week and you'll never succumb to the siren song of an expensive noodle bowl again.

build a bowl

FOLLOW THIS FORMULA TO BUILD DELICIOUS, HEALTHY NOODLE BOWLS THAT ARE EASIER THAN DECIDING WHERE TO GO FOR LUNCH

1 PICK A NOODLE

We like to keep things on the lighter side by going with naturally gluten-free Asian rice noodles, but any noodle will work here. Cook them according to the package directions—on Asian noodle packages there's usually a cooking time for stir-frying and for soups; go for the stir-fry time—then rinse well in cold water and toss with a bit of oil to prevent sticking.

2 GRAB A PROTEIN

The beautiful thing about noodle bowls is that you can do whatever your heart desires. The proteins in the recipes on page 89 are our go-tos, but when we're feeling lazy, we just top ours with store-bought deep-fried tofu or shredded rotisserie chicken. Or we'll boil, poach, or fry a couple of eggs and throw those on top with some fridge leftovers.

3 LOTS OF VEGETABLES

Double up on the seasonal vegetables and include both raw and cooked. Here are some of our favorites:

Raw: baby gem lettuce, arugula, baby spinach, baby kale, romaine, radicchio, matchstick carrots, sliced bell peppers, chopped tomatoes, thinly sliced onions, cucumber slices, shredded cabbage, shelled edamame, snap peas, snow peas, thinly sliced daikon, and, of course, avocado

Cooked: sautéed mushrooms, roasted beets; roasted Brussels sprouts, eggplant, parsnips, potatoes, sweet potatoes, squashes, and other root vegetables; blanched asparagus, broccoli, cauliflower, corn, and peas

4 TOSS IN SAUCE

We've included recipes for some of our favorite dressings on page 88, but really, any sauce will do. Look in your fridge for some inspiration. Pesto, harissa, chili oil (see page 53), and XO Sauce (see page 224) would all be great places to start playing around.

5 THE TOPPINGS MAKE THE BOWL

A great bowl of noodles is in the toppings, so try to get one of each category:

Sprouts: mung bean, lentil, chickpea, alfalfa, microgreens
Fresh herbs: sliced green onions, cilantro, mint, dill
Seeds, nuts, and other crunchy bits: toasted sesame seeds, pepitas, toasted sunflower seeds, hazelnuts, walnuts, almonds, toasted seaweed, Japanese pickles, kimchi

5 Great Dressings
Each makes about ½ cup (serves 4)

Garlic Miso Mustard

Whisk together 1 tablespoon miso, 1 tablespoon Dijon or whole grain mustard, ¼ cup neutral oil, 1 tablespoon toasted sesame oil, the juice of ½ lemon, and 1 clove of pressed or minced garlic in a medium bowl. Taste and season with salt and freshly ground black pepper.

Dashi-Soy

Combine 6 tablespoons soy sauce, 2 tablespoons sake, and 2 tablespoons mirin in a small saucepan over low heat. When the mixture bubbles, remove from the heat and add ½ cup of bonito flakes. Let sit for 1 hour at room temperature or, for a stronger dressing, overnight in the fridge. Strain before using.

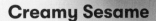

Spicy Fish Sauce

Finely mince 1 garlic clove and 1 Thai chili. Transfer to a small bowl and whisk in 2 tablespoons sugar, the juice of ½ lime, 2 tablespoons fish sauce, and ½ cup of water. Taste and adjust the ingredients as needed.

Creamy Sesame

Whisk together ¼ cup neutral oil, 2 tablespoons Chinese sesame paste (tahini will work too), 1 tablespoon rice vinegar, 2 teaspoons soy sauce, 2 teaspoons toasted sesame oil, 1 teaspoon sugar, and 1 clove of pressed or minced garlic. Taste and adjust the ingredients as needed.

Lemon Honey Mustard

Whisk together ½ cup olive oil, the juice of 2 lemons (about ¼ cup), 2 teaspoons honey, 2 teaspoons Dijon mustard, and optionally 4 tablespoons chopped fresh herbs of choice (parsley, chives, cilantro, dill) in a medium bowl. Taste and season with salt and freshly ground black pepper.

Proteins and Vegetables

Each serves 4

Lemongrass Chicken

Finely mince 1 stalk of lemongrass, 1 small shallot, and 2 cloves of garlic. Mix with 2 teaspoons sugar, 1 tablespoon fish sauce, and ½ teaspoon freshly ground black pepper. Add 1 pound of boneless chicken and marinate for 1 hour at room temperature (or overnight in the fridge). Heat up a bit of neutral oil in a nonstick skillet over medium heat and cook the chicken, flipping once, until cooked through, 8 to 12 minutes for breasts, 10 to 15 minutes for thighs. Let cool, then slice into ½-inch-thick slices.

Honey Garlic Tofu

Drain 1 package (14 to 16 ounces) of medium-firm tofu on a couple of paper towels, then cut into 1½-inch cubes. Toss to coat with 1 tablespoon cornstarch, shaking off the excess. Heat a bit of neutral oil in a nonstick skillet over medium-high heat, add the tofu, and fry until golden on all sides, flipping as needed, 8 to 10 minutes. Remove the tofu from the pan. Add 2 cloves of minced garlic, 1½ tablespoons honey, and 1 teaspoon soy sauce to the pan and cook, stirring, over low heat. Add the tofu back into the pan and toss to coat. Season with freshly ground black pepper and remove from the heat.

Simply Poached Salmon

Season 1 pound of scaled, boned, skin-on salmon fillets on both sides with salt and freshly ground black pepper. Combine 2 cups chicken stock or dashi (see page 236) with 2 sliced shallots, 2 tablespoons mirin, 2 tablespoons soy sauce, and 2 tablespoons sake in a medium sauté pan. Bring to a simmer over medium heat. Add the salmon fillets to the pan, cover, and cook until the salmon flakes easily, 5 to 10 minutes. Remove from the pan.

How to Roast Almost Any Vegetable

Wash and roughly chop about 4 cups of your favorite vegetables. Toss in oil, season with salt and freshly ground black pepper, and roast in a single layer on a rimmed baking sheet in a 425°F oven until tender, slightly crispy, and charred. Root vegetables will take 45 minutes to an hour; softer vegetables like green beans and broccoli will take 10 to 15 minutes. Leftovers can be refrigerated in an airtight container for up to 5 days.

Beijing's signature noodle is zha jiang mian, or fried sauce noodles. The sauce is a complex savory pork mix flavored with two types of Chinese bean sauce: sweet bean sauce and ground bean sauce. The two sauces are essential—they're full of sweet and salty umami goodness. Both are made with fermented yellow soybeans, but they're at opposite ends of the taste spectrum, with sweet bean sauce being sweet and ground bean sauce being salty. You can find both online or at your friendly local Asian grocery store. We like this sauce with all kinds of noodles (and it's traditionally served with wheat noodles), but perhaps our favorite is an extra-wide pasta noodle—pappardelle is always in our pantry and the sauce clings perfectly to the wide ribbons. A plate (or bowl) of these saucy, savory noodles topped with fresh and crunchy cucumber to contrast the richness is the perfect balance between taste and texture.

LEGENDARY ZHA JIANG MIAN

CHINESE BOLOGNESE PAPPARDELLE

1 tablespoon neutral oil

1 small shallot, peeled and minced

4 cloves garlic, peeled and pressed or minced

1 pound ground pork

¼ cup sweet bean sauce

2 tablespoons ground bean sauce

2 tablespoons sweet soy sauce (see Note)

Salt

12 ounces dried pappardelle

1. Heat the oil in a medium pot over medium-high heat. Add the shallot and garlic and cook until fragrant, about 1 minute. Stir in the pork and cook, breaking it up with a wooden spoon, until cooked through, 5 to 6 minutes.

2. Stir in both bean sauces, the sweet soy sauce, and ½ cup water. Simmer until slightly thick, about 10 minutes.

3. Meanwhile, bring a large pot of lightly salted water to a boil over high heat. Add the pappardelle and cook according to the package directions until it is al dente. Drain well, then return the pappardelle to the pot, add the sauce to taste, and toss.

4. Transfer the pappardelle to a family-style platter and serve.

Note: Sweet soy sauce is a thicker and sweeter version of dark soy sauce and can be found in any Asian grocery store. If you can't find it, here's an easy substitute: Gently heat 2 tablespoons of soy sauce in a small saucepan and add 1 teaspoon sugar, stirring until it dissolves.

tip! Sauce the noodles in batches and taste as you go; this sauce is salt-forward.

Serves 4

Toppings

Smashed or sliced cucumber
Sliced green onions
Chopped fresh cilantro
Ground white pepper
Crispy fried shallots (see page 239)

Make It Ahead

Make a batch of sauce and keep it in the fridge for midnight hunger pangs—just boil noodles and toss them with sauce to taste for a satisfying snack. The sauce will keep in an airtight container for to 2 to 3 days.

This is our take on classic moules frites, or Belgian mussels and fries. We switched out the fries for casarecce noodles (which are short twists of pasta that kind of look like fries if you squint) but kept the white wine, shallots, and butter that traditionally sauce the mussels. A bit of saffron adds a gorgeous golden-orange color to the dish. When buying the mussels, choose the freshest you can find: Pick shiny, unbroken, tightly closed shells or shells that close when lightly tapped. Don't forget to leave the bag open on the way home—they need air to stay alive.

NOODLES OVER FRIES ALWAYS

CASARECCE MOULES FRITES—HOLD THE FRITES

Serves 4

Toppings
Crispy Garlic
 Breadcrumbs
 (page 113)
Crushed red pepper
 flakes
Finely chopped fresh
 parsley

tip!

Whole saffron threads are better than ground, which can sometimes be cut with other fillers. When shopping, look for fine, even threads with a tiny trumpet-like flute on one end.

Salt

4 tablespoons (½ stick)
 unsalted butter

1 pinch (about 20)
 saffron threads

2 shallots, peeled and
 sliced

1 cup dry white wine

3 tablespoons finely
 chopped fresh flat-leaf
 parsley

Freshly ground black
 pepper

2½ pounds mussels,
 well scrubbed and
 debearded

12 ounces dried
 casarecce

½ lemon, thinly sliced

1. Bring a large pot of salted water to a boil over high heat.

2. Meanwhile, melt the butter in a large, deep sauté pan or Dutch oven over medium heat. Add the saffron and shallots and cook until the shallots are soft, stirring occasionally, 1 to 2 minutes. Add the wine and 1 tablespoon of the parsley and bring to a simmer. Season with salt and pepper, then add the mussels. Cover the pan tightly and steam the mussels until they open, lightly shaking the pan occasionally to ensure even cooking, about 5 minutes. Open the pan and discard any mussels that did not open. Use a slotted spoon to transfer the remaining mussels into a bowl. Cover with aluminum foil.

3. Add the casarecce to the boiling water and cook according to the package directions until it is 3 minutes shy of al dente. Drain well, reserving 1½ cups of the pasta cooking water.

4. Add ¼ cup of the pasta water to the saffron broth over high heat and whisk to emulsify, about 1 minute. Add the pasta and toss gently until it is al dente and the sauce becomes thick and glossy, about 3 minutes. Adjust the seasoning and add pasta water as needed to loosen the sauce.

5. Remove from the heat and add half of the mussels to the pasta along with any juices that have collected in the bowl. Add the remaining 2 tablespoons parsley and the lemon slices. Toss well to mix, then top with the remaining mussels. Serve immediately.

Dan dan noodles are the ultimate convergence of spice, meat, and noodles. One taste and you'll get why they're the most popular noodles from Sichuan. There are plenty of dan dan noodles that call for just chili oil and sesame paste. We upped the ante a little here with doubanjiang—a Chinese spicy bean paste made from a blend of chilies and fermented soy and broad beans—which gives this particular dan dan a salty, spicy, complex Sichuan flavor. With its reddish-brown hue and rich, complex umami, doubanjiang is fondly referred to as the soul of Sichuan cuisine.

THE UMAMI BOMB

SPICY PORK SICHUAN DAN DAN MIAN

2 teaspoons neutral oil

1 shallot, peeled and diced

4 cloves garlic, peeled and pressed or minced

½ pound ground pork

2 teaspoons Shaoxing wine (see page 235)

2 teaspoons hoisin sauce

1 teaspoon toasted sesame oil

2 tablespoons light soy sauce

2 tablespoons doubanjiang (see page 237)

1 tablespoon chili oil (preferably homemade; see page 53)

2 tablespoons Chinese sesame paste (see page 236)

1 tablespoon Chinese black vinegar (see page 236)

1 tablespoon sugar

12 ounces Chinese oil noodles (see page 12) or a long pasta

1. Heat the neutral oil in a large sauté pan over medium heat. When the oil is hot and shimmering, add the shallot and garlic and cook, stirring occasionally, until soft but not brown, 1 to 2 minutes. Add the ground pork and stir-fry until the pork is brown and crispy, 4 to 5 minutes. Stir in the Shaoxing wine, hoisin, sesame oil, and 1 tablespoon of the soy sauce. Remove the pan from the heat and use a slotted spoon to remove the pork to a plate; set it aside.

2. Return the pan to the stove and turn the heat to medium-low. Add the doubanjiang and cook, stirring, until heated through, 1 to 2 minutes. Add ¼ cup of water to the pan, stirring to scrape up any browned bits, then remove the pan from the heat and stir in the remaining 1 tablespoon of soy sauce and the chili oil, sesame paste, vinegar, and sugar until dissolved. Set aside.

3. Bring a large pot of water to a boil over high heat. Cook the noodles according to the package directions. Drain well, reserving 1 cup of the noodle cooking water. Transfer the noodles to the sauce in the pan and toss gently over medium heat, thinning with some reserved noodle water if the sauce looks too dry.

4. Top the noodles with the pork and serve hot.

Serves 4

Toppings
Sliced green onions
Chopped fresh cilantro
Toasted sesame seeds
Chili oil

tip!

If you can't find authentic doubanjiang, Lee Kum Kee makes a more Cantonese-style chili bean sauce called toban djan that will work in a pinch.

Briny, bright, and fresh, capers are the backbone of this dish. These tiny green pods can be polarizing, but that's because they're often prepared incorrectly. Cooking them in garlicky butter slowly over low heat allows their flavors to mellow and release, leaving a tiny pop of salty tartness that goes well with seafood (and pretty much everything else). When you think you need more salt or pepper, often what you really need is capers. Here we use calamarata pasta, a wide, circular pasta that looks like calamari (hence the name), but feel free to use your favorite short pasta. We just like visual puns.

THE SEAFOOD TOWER

CALAMARATA WITH SHRIMP AND SCALLOPS

1 pound large shrimp, peeled and deveined

1 pound bay scallops

Salt and freshly ground black pepper

2 tablespoons olive oil

12 ounces dried calamarata or other short pasta

4 tablespoons (½ stick) unsalted butter

10 cloves garlic, peeled and sliced

1 tablespoon capers, drained

½ cup dry white wine

½ cup finely grated Parmigiano-Reggiano cheese

Juice of ½ lemon

3 tablespoons finely chopped fresh flat-leaf parsley

1. Pat the shrimp and scallops dry with paper towels and season on both sides with salt and pepper. Heat the oil in a large sauté pan over high heat. Add the shrimp and scallops, working in batches if necessary to avoid crowding the pan, and sear, flipping once, until golden brown, 1 to 3 minutes per side depending on size. Transfer to a bowl and reserve. Set aside the pan (no need to wash it) for Step 3.

2. Bring a large pot of salted water to a boil over high heat. Add the calamarata and cook according to the package directions until it is 3 minutes shy of al dente. Drain well, reserving 1½ cups of the pasta cooking water.

3. Return the sauté pan to low heat, add the butter, and let it melt, then add the garlic and capers. Cook, stirring occasionally, until the garlic is soft and fragrant but not brown, 3 to 4 minutes. Turn the heat up to medium-high and add the wine. Let simmer until reduced by half, 2 to 3 minutes. Add ¾ cup of the pasta water to the pan (it will bubble up a bit) and bring to a gentle boil, whisking to emulsify and scrape up any browned bits on the bottom of the pan, about 1 minute.

4. Add the calamarata to the pan and cook, tossing occasionally, until it is al dente and the sauce reduces and becomes thick and glossy, about 3 minutes. Remove the pan from the heat and stir in the cheese until it's melted, thinning out the sauce with reserved pasta water if needed. Stir in the lemon juice and parsley, then add the seafood and any juices that have collected in the bowl. Adjust the seasoning to taste. Adjust the seasoning to taste and serve.

Serves 4

Toppings

Crispy Garlic Breadcrumbs (page 113)
Finely grated Parmigiano
Crushed red pepper flakes

tip!

Be sure to keep an eye on the shrimp and scallops without depending on a timer; they will finish cooking—and should be removed from the pan—at different times.

If you are nervous about cooking scallops, it's easy: Make sure your skillet is very hot, use plenty of oil, and give them space in the pan so they're not steaming next to each other. Sear them without moving for the first minute or two, then peek at the bottom of the first one you set into the pan. If the bottom is golden, flip it and proceed with the remaining scallops. That's all there is to it!

NOODLE FUN FOR EVERYONE

4

CHILL PARTY AND POTLUCK NOODLES

Is it really a party without noodles?

We say no. We've kept these larger-format noodle party dishes on the more affordable side so you can feed all your friends without breaking the bank. The proteins in these recipes are relatively simple: Think packs of bacon, cans of (high-quality) tuna and sardines, tofu, and pork shoulder. At our house, noodles and good friends always equal a fun time. It's time to gather around and slurp and socialize the night away. These recipes are all standardized to serve four people generously, but if you're feeding a larger group, they will always double, triple, or x-tuple easily.

In the afternoons and evenings at taquerias and taco trucks across Mexico and the American Southwest, you'll see stacks of sliced, marinated pork shoulder layered on giant vertical spits, topped with a pineapple and slow-roasting away. As the flames cook and char the edges of the meat, a chef with a wickedly sharp knife slices off crispy, smoky, sweet shards directly into a waiting tortilla. Often, a piece of roasted pineapple will be sliced off and expertly caught midair, finishing the show with a flourish.

We love tacos and we love noodles and we love them together even more. The hardest part of making great tacos at home is finding high-quality tortillas like those made in Sonora, California, or Mexico. This yakiudon al pastor does away with that problem entirely, combining chewy fried udon noodles with our smoky slow-roasted pork al pastor. It's a fairy-tale marriage for the ages.

LET'S TACO 'BOUT NOODLES

OVEN-ROASTED YAKIUDON AL PASTOR

8 dried guajillo chiles, stemmed and seeded (see Notes)

8 cloves garlic, peeled

1 can (7 ounces) chipotle chiles in adobo

2 tablespoons sugar

2 tablespoons achiote paste (see Notes)

1 can (about 14 ounces) pineapple rings in natural juice (juice reserved)

2 pounds boneless pork shoulder, cut crosswise into ¼-inch-thick slices

Salt

½ red onion, peeled and roughly chopped

Juice of 2 limes

½ cup chopped fresh cilantro

4 bricks frozen Sanuki-style udon noodles (about 8 ounces each; see Notes)

2 tablespoons neutral oil

1. Soak the guajillos in a small bowl filled with hot tap water until soft, 15 minutes.

2. Place the guajillos in a blender along with the garlic, chipotles, sugar, achiote paste, and ½ cup of the reserved pineapple juice. Blend into a smooth marinade.

3. Season the pork generously with salt, then place it in a large ziplock bag and add the marinade. Seal it and turn the bag a few times to coat. Let marinate at room temperature for at least 30 minutes and up to 2 hours.

4. Meanwhile, heat your oven to 500°F with a rack set to the middle position. Line a rimmed baking sheet with aluminum foil, then arrange ½ cup of the pineapple chunks in a single layer on the foil. Broil until the edges start to char, about 15 minutes. Remove from the oven (leave the oven on for the next step).

5. Chop the roasted pineapple, then transfer to a medium bowl and combine with the red onion, lime juice, and cilantro to make a salsa. Season to taste with salt and set it aside.

6. Line a sheet pan with aluminum foil and arrange the pork (with the marinade) in the pan in as close to a single layer as possible. Broil the pork until the edges and corners start to char, about 20 minutes.

Serves 4

Make It Ahead

The pineapple salsa can be prepared in advance and stored in an airtight container in the fridge for up to 2 days. The pork can also be marinated 2 hours ahead of time. When you are ready to cook, proceed with the recipe as directed from Step 6.

Continued on next page ⟶

tip!

This al pastor recipe works perfectly for taco night, too. We like to make a double portion and have the best of both worlds.

If you like your salsa on the spicy side (we do), add one or two sliced chiles of your choice to the salsa before you mix it up.

7. While the pork broils, fill a large bowl with hot tap water and add the frozen udon. Once the noodles are loosened and warmed through, 2 to 3 minutes, drain well.

8. When the pork is done, remove it from the oven and set it aside. Heat a large nonstick skillet or high-sided pot over high heat, then add the oil. When the oil starts to shimmer, add the loosened udon, the pork, and any juices in the baking pan and stir-fry until the noodles are coated in sauce and the pork is completely cooked through, 3 to 4 minutes. (You may need to work in batches if your skillet is not large enough.) Serve immediately, topped with the pineapple salsa.

Notes: The dried guajillos can be a little hard to find if you don't have a large supermarket or Latin foods market nearby, but you can substitute any dried chiles if you can't find these exact ones. You may want to remove some or all of the seeds to reduce the heat.

Achiote paste is a classic Latin American seasoning that's sold in standard-size bricks in the Latin foods aisle at most major supermarkets, at Latin foods stores, and online. We like El Yucateco, which is a widely available brand.

The best available udon is frozen Sanuki-style udon, imported directly from Japan. It's the closest you'll get to fresh. The noodles, which are cooked and then flash-frozen, are firm and chewy, with just the right amount of slippery supple bite.

When the weather turns chilly and we're looking for a wholesome, warming dish, we turn to this lamb ragu. Bone-in lamb shoulder chops are slow-cooked with wine and tomatoes for a satisfying sauce that's surprisingly easy to make. Fresh mint and peas, whether fresh or frozen, add bright pops of green to cut through the richness of the lamb. Braises are the way to go when dinner partying; they're hands-off and hearty. We use reginette, a long ribbon-like pasta, with this sauce, but any flat, wide noodle will work.

Luxe Lamb Ragu

SLOW-BRAISED LAMB AND PEAS WITH REGINETTE

2 pounds bone-in lamb shoulder chops (3 to 5 chops)

Salt and freshly ground black pepper

2 tablespoons neutral oil

¼ cup chopped guanciale

1 medium onion, peeled and diced

1 carrot, diced

1 celery rib, diced

1½ cups dry white wine

3 tablespoons tomato paste

2 to 3 cups sodium-free beef stock

12 ounces dried reginette

1 cup fresh or frozen English peas

⅓ cup chopped fresh mint

1. Lightly pat both sides of the lamb chops dry with a paper towel and season generously all over with salt and pepper.

2. Heat the oil in a large Dutch oven or heavy-bottomed pot over medium-high heat until hot and shimmery. Add the chops and sear, turning occasionally, until deeply browned on all sides, 5 to 6 minutes. Transfer the chops to a plate and set aside.

3. Reduce the heat to medium and add the guanciale to the pot. Cook, stirring, until browned, 2 to 3 minutes. Stir in the onion, carrot, and celery and cook until soft but not browned, 1 to 2 minutes. Pour in the wine, stirring and scraping the bottom of the pot to release any browned bits, and let simmer until reduced by half, 1 to 2 minutes. Stir in the tomato paste.

4. Return the lamb to the pot along with enough beef stock to cover. When bubbles start to break the surface of the liquid, reduce the heat to low, partially cover the pot with a lid, and braise until the lamb is pull-apart fork-tender, about 2 hours.

5. When you're almost ready to serve, bring a large pot of salted water to a boil over high heat. Meanwhile, remove the lamb from the sauce, shred or chop the meat (discard the bones and any large pieces of fat), and then stir it back into the sauce. Keep the sauce warm on low heat while you wait for the pasta to cook.

Serves 4

Toppings

Crispy Garlic Breadcrumbs (page 113)
Crushed red pepper flakes
Finely grated Parmigiano

Make It Ahead

Double this ragu and freeze half in an airtight container for up to a month. Future You will thank Past You.

Continued on page 107 ———————➤

6. Add the reginette to the boiling water and cook according to the package directions until it is 3 minutes shy of al dente. Drain well, reserving 1 cup of the pasta cooking water.

7. Transfer the reginette to the pot with the lamb sauce and cook over medium heat, stirring, for 1 minute. Add the peas and cook, stirring, until the sauce clings to the pasta, the pasta is al dente, and the peas are cooked (frozen peas will cook almost immediately), 1 to 2 minutes. If the sauce seems thick, add reserved pasta water ¼ cup at a time until it reaches your desired consistency.

8. Remove from the heat and stir in the mint. Serve immediately.

Back in the days after the Korean War, when there was not a lot of food to go around, Koreans invented this hearty, over-the-top spicy stew using the food the US army left behind. This is one of our favorite things to make on a lazy-yet-social night when we're hanging out with longtime friends. Army stew is hot pot culture at its finest, and it gets better as the night goes on and the flavors meld and more food is added. You can use the add-ons we suggest in the box below, but feel free to throw in anything you like. This dish is meant to be customized to your taste—just don't forget the noodles!

THE MESS HALL

LIKE FONDUE BUT IT'S KOREAN ARMY STEW

Serves 4

Toppings

Sliced green onions
Toasted sesame seeds

5x Better

Crisp up the hot dogs (and Spam, if using—see box below) for some textural interest. They sear nicely in a large skillet over medium-high heat.

tip!

This stew is best enjoyed hot and bubbling. We like to use a portable burner or induction cooker and keep the stew simmering on low at the table, with everyone sharing tongs and scoops to pick out as much or as little as they'd like to place in small bowls. When the stew starts to run low, we add more packs of instant noodles and chicken stock, let it come back up to a boil, and keep on eating. Pro tip: Keep a pair of clean scissors around to cut the noodles as you pull them out of the stew, so things don't get too messy.

2 tablespoons gochujang (see page 236)

2 tablespoons mirin

1 tablespoon soy sauce

1 tablespoon sugar

½ teaspoon freshly ground black pepper

2 tablespoons Korean red pepper flakes (optional)

4 cloves garlic, peeled and crushed

4 cups sodium-free chicken stock

1 cup chopped kimchi

4 hot dogs, sliced diagonally

1 cup sliced king oyster mushrooms

1 cup sliced carrots

2 packages instant ramen, seasoning packets discarded

1 or 2 large eggs (optional)

1 or 2 slices American cheese

1. Make the broth: Stir together the gochujang, mirin, soy sauce, sugar, black pepper, red pepper flakes (if using), and garlic in a wide, shallow pot with a lid. Pour in the chicken stock and add the kimchi.

2. Arrange the hot dogs in the pot. Partially cover with a lid, bring to a boil over medium-high heat, and let simmer for 8 to 10 minutes.

3. Remove the lid and add the mushrooms, carrots, and instant ramen. Crack in the egg(s), if using. Simmer until the vegetables are tender and the noodles are cooked, 3 minutes.

4. Top with the cheese slices and let melt slightly before digging in. Serve family-style, with scoops, chopsticks, tongs, a small bowl for each person, and lots of drinks.

We have a handful of favorite add-ons for this hearty stew: sliced Spam, sliced medium-firm tofu, mini tofu puffs, and broccoli. If you're a first timer, we highly recommend starting with these toppings, and then adding whatever else strikes your fancy, such as sliced pork shoulder, bacon, bite-size pieces of chicken, Korean fish balls, Korean rice cake, cabbage, kale, cherry tomatoes, sliced bell peppers, or even frozen corn. The sky's the limit! Add meats and sliced tofu along with the hot dogs in Step 2, and tofu puffs and any additional veggies in Step 3.

Bacon and kimchi go together like mac and cheese or burgers and fries, so it's no surprise that we took the classic Korean combination and used the flavors as the backbone of this smoky, spicy yakiudon. Something magical happens when you cook kimchi with bacon—the kimchi melts and mellows out, leaving a pleasantly complex, slightly spicy, addictive "I need more" feeling. Pair this with copious amounts of Korean *soju*, sake, white wine, or beer and a good time is guaranteed.

UDON WANNA MISS THIS

SMOKY BACON KIMCHI FRIED UDON

1 pound bacon (preferably thick cut)

4 bricks (8 ounces each) frozen Sanuki-style udon (see Notes, page 104)

1 bunch kale, stemmed and torn into 2- to 3-inch pieces

2 cups chopped kimchi, plus ¼ cup kimchi juice from the jar

4 tablespoons (½ stick) unsalted butter

3 tablespoons gochujang (see page 236)

1. Cook the bacon in batches in a large nonstick skillet over medium heat until brown and crispy, flipping as needed, 6 to 10 minutes. As it's done, transfer the bacon to a plate lined with paper towels. Slice the bacon into 1-inch squares and set aside. Drain off all but 1 tablespoon of the rendered fat in the pan.

2. Meanwhile, fill a large bowl with hot tap water and add the frozen udon. Once the noodles are loosened and warmed through, 2 to 3 minutes, drain well and set aside.

3. Return the pan to medium heat and add the kale and chopped kimchi. Cook, stirring occasionally, until the kale is soft and the kimchi is slightly caramelized, 2 to 3 minutes. Add the butter and gochujang, stirring to melt the butter. Mix everything into an even sauce, then remove the pan from the heat.

4. Add the noodles and bacon to the kale mixture in the pan, then add the kimchi juice. Set over low heat and cook, tossing, until the noodles are coated and glossy, 1 to 2 minutes. Serve hot.

Serves 4

Toppings

Nori seaweed strips
Sliced green onions
Toasted sesame seeds

5x Better

Throw an egg on it—top off each bowl with a raw egg yolk (see Note, page 21), scrambled egg, or other egg preparation of your choice for a rich counterpoint to the kimchi.

MAKING YOUR OWN

BREADCRUMBS

IS THE SECRET TO AMAZING PASTA

Homemade garlic breadcrumbs will change your life. Dramatic, but true. Once you go homemade, you'll never go back. A fresh breadcrumb is so much more than store-bought. Think of it like a tiny piece of perfectly toasted toast, with loads of craggy edges for butter and garlic to nestle into. The type of bread you use here is not important; use your favorite kind or experiment. We like breadcrumbs so much that sometimes we buy a strange new loaf just to breadcrumb it up. Add breadcrumbs to any and every noodle for an extra bit of crunch and flavor.

ARE YOU A SQUARE?
Cut your bread into perfect cubes—they're tiny little forkable garlic breads, perfect with spaghetti and meatballs (see page 33) or with any of the other pastas, such as the Luxe Lamb Ragu (page 105).

WILD AND FREE
Use a food processor to blitz bread into un-even pieces to make a coarse mix of largish pieces and mini panko-size ones—the big crumbs are satisfyingly crispy and the little ones cling to noodles for a crunchy hug.

Crispy Garlic Breadcrumps

1 tablespoon unsalted
   butter

1 tablespoon olive oil

1 cup fresh breadcrumbs

2 or 3 cloves garlic,
   peeled and pressed
   or minced

Salt and freshly ground
   black pepper

1. Heat the butter and oil in a large nonstick frying pan over medium heat until the butter melts.

2. Add the breadcrumbs and stir to coat evenly. Turn the heat up to medium-high and toast, stirring frequently, until the breadcrumbs are lightly golden, about 3 minutes. Add the garlic and continue to cook until the breadcrumbs are toasty, 1 to 2 more minutes.

3. Remove from the heat and season to taste with salt and pepper. Enjoy warm or let cool completely and store in an airtight container in the fridge for up to 1 week.

Makes 1 cup

CRISPY AND CHEESY BREADCRUMBS
Like the best bits of a grilled cheese. Add 2 tablespoons finely grated Parmigiano-Reggiano or pecorino Romano cheese to the pan when you add the bread-crumbs.

HERBY BREADCRUMBS
Green herby freshness. Stir in chopped herbs (parsley, rosemary, thyme, chives, sage) after you remove the bread-crumbs from the heat.

CRISPY CHILI BREADCRUMBS
Add these for a bit of heat. Stir in ¼ teaspoon crushed red pepper flakes with the garlic.

This is one of those dishes you won't believe came mostly out of a can, but it's true. With all the access to fresh produce and seafood these days, this dish is a nice way to celebrate how important canning and preservation used to be. Like good dried pasta, quality canned fish has a unique texture all its own that can't be reproduced with the fresh stuff. The trick is to use the best canned or jarred tuna you can find, preferably something from Italy or elsewhere in the Mediterranean. Look for something that still looks like fish when you open the can—the difference between a really good and just average canned fish cannot be overstated.

CHITARRA AL TONNO

CANNED FISH *CAN* TASTE THIS GOOD

Salt

2 tablespoons olive oil

6 to 8 cloves garlic, peeled and sliced

¼ cup chopped fresh flat-leaf parsley

8 anchovy fillets

1 cup canned crushed tomatoes

1 tablespoon capers, rinsed

16 Niçoise or other cured black olives, pitted

8 ounces high-quality tuna in olive oil, drained and flaked

4 portions (24 ounces total) Spaghetti alla Chitarra (page 13) or fresh pasta of your choice

Freshly ground black pepper

1. Bring a large pot of salted water to a boil over high heat.

2. Meanwhile, heat the oil in a large sauté pan over medium-high heat. When the oil is hot, add the garlic, parsley, and anchovies and cook, stirring often so that the parsley doesn't burn, until combined and cooked down slightly, about 1 minute. Stir in the crushed tomatoes and simmer until reduced by half, about 5 minutes. Add the capers, olives, and flaked tuna and mix well.

3. Add the spaghetti to the boiling water and cook until it just starts to float, 2 to 3 minutes. Drain well, reserving 1 cup of the pasta cooking water.

4. Add the pasta to the sauce and cook, stirring occasionally, until the sauce is glossy and the spaghetti is al dente, 2 to 3 minutes. Loosen the sauce with some of the reserved pasta water, adding it ¼ cup at a time, if the spaghetti looks dry.

5. Taste and season with salt and pepper. Serve immediately.

Serves 4

Toppings

Crispy Garlic Breadcrumbs (page 113)
Chopped olives
Chopped fresh flat-leaf parsley
Crushed red pepper flakes

If you really feel like splurging, try to find Italian canned tuna belly—it's the same stuff used in toro sushi. You don't even have to stop at tuna—canned mackerel, or even salmon, makes for an amazing variation. Although it's not as traditional, Japanese canned fish, whether canned with salt or miso, can be another delicious option.

Even though the name of this dish technically translates to "bucatini with sardines," the real magic is in the fennel. This recipe is based on a classic Sardinian combination of foraged wild fennel, bright sweet golden raisins, and crispy breadcrumbs. If you manage to make this in summer, visit your local farmers market and try to find wild fennel, but even regular grocery store fennel will make this a special, standout dish with unique flavors not usually found in Italian cuisine. Be sure to get a fennel bulb with fronds still attached. Like the Chitarra al Tonno on page 115, this is one of those dishes where the quality of the canned fish makes a big difference, so go for the good, slightly more expensive Spanish or Italian sardines packed in olive oil.

BUCATINI CON LE SARDE

CANNED FISH CAN TASTE THIS GOOD, TOO

Serves 4

Toppings

Crispy Garlic
  Breadcrumbs
  (page 113)
Golden raisins

5x Better

Add a pinch of saffron to the sauce while it's simmering to get that classic golden color.

tip!

Some grocery stores chop off all or most of a fennel bulb's fronds as the vegetable ages and its fronds wither (they may look terrible, but the bulb is still okay to eat—and sell). A higher-end grocery store will probably have a fennel bulb with more than enough fronds, but if your bulb doesn't have enough fronds to fill ¼ cup, don't stress, the recipe will still taste good!

Salt

1 bunch fennel, trimmed, bulb roughly chopped, fronds reserved

12 ounces dried bucatini

¼ cup olive oil

8 ounces high-quality sardines, packed in olive oil

6 to 8 cloves garlic, peeled and sliced

1 tablespoon capers, rinsed

¼ cup golden raisins

8 anchovy fillets

1. Bring a large pot of salted water to a boil over high heat. Add the fennel fronds and blanch for 1 minute, then remove with a slotted spoon and drain on a paper towel. Add the bucatini to the boiling water and cook according to the package directions until it is 3 minutes shy of al dente. Drain well, reserving 1½ cups of the pasta cooking water.

2. Meanwhile, heat the olive oil in a large sauté pan over medium heat until it's shimmering, then add the sardines and fry until they are lightly crisped and warmed through, about 2 minutes. Remove from the pan and set aside.

3. Add the garlic to the pan and cook, stirring, until just fragrant, being careful not to let the garlic burn, about 30 seconds. Add ½ cup of the chopped fennel bulb along with the capers, raisins, anchovies, and 1 cup of the pasta water. Reduce the heat to low and simmer until the fennel is soft and translucent, 8 to 10 minutes.

4. While the sauce is simmering, chop enough fennel fronds to fill ¼ cup. (Save the rest of the fennel fronds for topping and the rest of the bulb for another use.) Break up the sardines into bite-size pieces with a spoon.

5. Add the bucatini to the simmering sauce and turn the heat up to medium-high. Cook, stirring gently, until the bucatini is al dente and the sauce has become glossy, adding more pasta water if necessary, about 3 minutes. Remove the pan from the heat.

6. Stir the chopped fennel fronds and sardine pieces into the pasta and serve immediately. Top with the reserved fennel fronds.

Kimchi, our favorite spicy fermented side dish, is the star of this ramen. Cooking it along with onions caramelizes and deepens the flavors, making it the perfect backbone for this slow-braised pork belly stock. This stew is the perfect party food: It's wonderful after two hours of cooking, but if you have time to make it ahead, it can simmer longer and the flavors will meld and intensify while you get ready and do other things. This is cold weather comfort food at its best: warming, hearty, and full of noodles.

FIVE STAR KIMCHI RAMEN

RAMEN WITH SLOW-BRAISED PORK BELLY KIMCHI STEW

1/4 cup neutral oil

2 medium onions, peeled and sliced

4 cups chopped napa cabbage kimchi with juices

12 cups dashi (see page 236)

6 tablespoons mirin, or to taste

1 pound pork belly

24 ounces fresh ramen noodles

Salt and freshly ground black pepper

1. Heat the oil in a large heavy-bottomed pot or Dutch oven over medium heat. Add the onions and cook, stirring every 2 minutes or so and being careful not to let them burn, until caramelized evenly to a medium-brown color, about 20 minutes.

2. Stir in the kimchi and cook until soft, 2 to 3 minutes. Add the dashi, mirin, and pork belly. Turn the heat up to high and bring the mixture to a boil, then reduce the heat to low and simmer, partially covered, until the pork is tender and cooked through, at least 1½ hours.

3. When you are ready to serve, bring a large pot of water to a boil over high heat. Meanwhile, remove the pork belly to a cutting board and slice it into 1/4-inch-thick slices; set aside. Add the noodles to the boiling water and cook according to the package directions. Drain well.

4. Season the stew to taste with salt and pepper. Ladle the hot broth into warmed bowls (about 2 cups per bowl). Divide the noodles among the bowls and top each with pieces of kimchi and sliced pork belly. Serve piping hot.

Variation: Superfast Kimchi Ramen

If you're in a hurry, slice the pork belly into 1/4-inch slices and fry it in the pot or Dutch oven over medium-high heat until golden and cooked through, 1 to 2 minutes per side. Remove the pork belly from the pot and use the rendered fat to caramelize the onions in Step 1. In Step 2, simmer the stew just long enough to let the flavors meld, 20 to 30 minutes, then skip right to Step 3.

Serves 4 to 6

Toppings

Ramen Eggs (page 217) or a raw egg yolk
Shredded lettuce or cabbage
Sliced mushrooms
Nori sheets
Korean chili thread

Make It Ahead

If you are making this ahead of time, keep the stew partially covered on a very low simmer, with a few gentle bubbles breaking the surface, for up to 6 hours, adding extra dashi ½ cup at a time if the stock gets too low.

HELLO
my name is

BUN CHA

Bun cha became a little bit famous after Anthony Bourdain and President Obama met in Vietnam and had it for dinner. Most people who first run into it are a little bit daunted about how to eat it, including President Obama himself. It's just like tsukemen, though: You take a little of everything and dip it into the sauce, then slurp to your heart's content. The magic of bun cha is in the marriage of the savory, sweet, and spicy sauce and the smoky charcoal-grilled meats. Some people (including us) believe that proper bun cha contains two types of meat: crispy pork and tender meatballs. It's the contrast in textures between the two that really makes the dish something special.

Bun cha is just about the easiest fancy noodle dish you'll ever make, and it's perfect for scaling up to feed dinner parties of all sizes. The focus is on fresh ingredients, smoky grilled meats, and an amazing fish sauce vinaigrette.

1 Vermicelli

It's easy to get confused when buying vermicelli, especially if you're shopping at an Asian supermarket, where you'll find thick and thin vermicelli, mung bean vermicelli, and more. We use a common thin rice vermicelli made by Golden Swallow that's available pretty much everywhere—it comes in a clear bag with a red label.

2 Fish Sauce Vinaigrette

In Vietnam, the belief is that a dish is nothing without a great fish sauce, and that's especially true for bun cha. Fish sauce vinaigrettes are usually closely guarded family recipes, and ours is no exception—but we've shared it here with you (see page 124). The secret is to go the extra mile, using a mortar and pestle to grind together the garlic-sugar-chili paste.

3 Crispy Pork Shoulder

The crispy pork shoulder is an essential not-to-be-missed part of the dish. It provides a hint of char to counterbalance the sweetness in the vinaigrette. We really love the contrast of textures between the bounciness of the meatballs and the crispiness of the shoulder as well.

4 Meatballs

These meatballs are the star of the dish. We marinate our ground pork in a caramel fish sauce for at least an hour before forming it into balls, and it's absolutely worth the extra time. The meatballs end up with an addictive texture that even holds up to being submerged in fish sauce vinaigrette.

5 Bean Sprouts

We use raw mung bean sprouts to get that signature crunch, but you can quickly blanch them if you prefer a milder taste and texture.

6 Cucumbers

Cucumbers provide a cooling fresh note. We use English (seedless) cucumbers and slice them on a slight bias.

7 Fresh Herbs

Bun cha includes herbs and leafy greens such as lettuce, mint, Thai basil, cilantro, shiso, and Vietnamese coriander (listed here in order of how easy each is to find). You can find Thai basil in clamshells in the herb section of most good supermarkets these days, but to get fresh shiso and Vietnamese coriander, you'll probably need to visit an Asian grocery store. If you can't find any, don't sweat it; even just lettuce is pretty great.

8 A Bowl

Bun cha typically comes on a (usually bamboo) tray with all the fixings and an empty bowl for each person. You use your chopsticks to grab a little vermicelli, some meat, and a pinch of herbs, then spoon over some of the fish sauce vinaigrette that seasons the meat. Eating it this way allows you to control the flavors and textures of each bite and keeps all of the ingredients fresher and crispier.

Bun cha is a sublime deconstructed vermicelli bun bowl traditionally served on large bamboo trays on the streets of Hanoi. It features charcoal-grilled pork meatballs and pork shoulder, a fragrant umami-rich fish sauce vinaigrette, and all the herbs you could ever want. It's spicy and smoky and undeniably addictive. Our version eschews the charcoal grill for an easier and more dependable oven-roasting method, but we've kept everything else about this classic Vietnamese dish the same—even the tray.

BUN CHA

CHARRED PORK MEATBALLS WITH VERMICELLI

Serves 4

Although the traditional way to serve this is on a tray and with many dishes, we offer family-style instructions here so you can avoid a lot of dishwashing. Should you own a dishwasher and enough dishes, though, serving bun cha individual-style is four times the fun!

2 tablespoons sugar

¼ cup fish sauce

2 tablespoons oyster sauce

2 shallots, peeled and minced

5 cloves garlic, peeled and pressed or minced

1 pound boneless pork shoulder, cut into ½-inch slices

1 pound ground pork

1 Thai chili, stemmed and sliced, plus extra whole chilies for serving

Juice of ½ lime

12 ounces thin rice vermicelli noodles

1 bunch fresh mint leaves, for serving

1 bunch fresh cilantro leaves, for serving

Sliced red or green leaf lettuce, for serving

2 cups mung bean sprouts, for serving

Thinly sliced English cucumber, for serving

1. Make a caramel by heating 1 tablespoon of water and 1 tablespoon of sugar together in a saucepan over medium-low heat, without stirring or disturbing it in any way. When the sugar starts to turn golden brown, remove the pan from the heat and swirl in another 2 tablespoons of water until the mixture turns a light brown color. Add 2 tablespoons of the fish sauce, the oyster sauce, the shallots, and 4 cloves of the garlic and mix well to combine.

2. Divide the caramel between two medium bowls or ziplock bags. Place the pork shoulder slices in one bowl and turn to coat them with the caramel; place the ground pork in the other and use your hands to massage the caramel into the pork. Let marinate at room temperature for 15 to 30 minutes.

3. Meanwhile, make the vinaigrette: Crush together the remaining clove of garlic, the Thai chili, and the remaining 1 tablespoon of sugar using a mortar and pestle (or mince the garlic and chili together, then add the sugar). Transfer to a small bowl and stir in 1 cup of water, the remaining 2 tablespoons of fish sauce, and the lime juice. Set aside.

4. Preheat your oven to 400°F. Line a rimmed baking sheet with aluminum foil.

5. Use your hands to form the ground pork mixture into slightly flattened meatballs (about ½ inch thick and 1 inch wide) and place them on the prepared baking sheet. Remove the sliced pork from the marinade (discard the marinade) and arrange it in a single layer around the meatballs (or on a second aluminum foil–lined baking sheet). Roast until the meatballs are slightly charred and the pork slices are cooked through, about 15 minutes.

6. While the meat is roasting, bring a large pot of water to a boil over high heat. Add the noodles and cook according to the package directions. Drain and rinse them in cold water, then transfer them to a large serving plate.

7. Divide the meatballs and sliced pork among four small bowls and top each with an equal amount of the fish sauce vinaigrette. Serve with the vermicelli, herbs, lettuce, bean sprouts, cucumber, and extra chilies alongside.

5x Better

Add pickled garlic and peppers to take this to the next level. Bring 1 cup of water to a boil in a small pot. Add ½ cup rice vinegar, 1 tablespoon sugar, 1 teaspoon salt, 1 head of garlic (cloves separated and peeled), and 1 to 2 stemmed, sliced Thai chilies. Turn off the heat and let stand for 1 hour. The pickles will keep in a jar in the fridge almost indefinitely, although your garlic may turn blue if it's very fresh (the garlic is still safe to eat if this happens).

HELLO
my name is

WOK NOODLES

Almost every Southeast Asian country has a version of noodles that we like to refer to as wok noodles. Basically, they're wok-fried noodles tossed in a dark sweet sauce, sometimes with mix-ins, sometimes without, always delicious. Super saucy, smoky, sweet, and savory, these wok noodles can go two ways: quick and easy or elaborate and over the top. If you're looking for quick and easy, make the sauce, toss with cooked noodles, and top with a fried egg. If you want just a little bit extra, go all the way and prepare a bunch of the mix-ins and toppings from the lists on the next page. And even if you don't own a wok, you can use a sauté pan and these will still be the best noodles ever.

WOK NOODLES

Make the Sauce

This recipe makes enough for 4 to 6 portions depending on how rich and saucy you prefer your noodles.

- 2 tablespoons neutral oil
- 4 cloves garlic, peeled and pressed or minced
- 2 tablespoons oyster sauce
- 2 tablespoons hoisin sauce
- 1 tablespoon soy sauce
- 1 tablespoon rice vinegar
- 1 tablespoon sugar
- Freshly ground black pepper, to taste

Heat the oil in a small saucepan over medium heat. Add the garlic and cook, stirring, until it is soft and fragrant, 1 to 2 minutes. Stir in the remaining ingredients and simmer for about 2 minutes. Remove from the heat. Taste and adjust the flavors if needed.

Fry Your Mix-Ins

Heat up a slick of oil in a wok over medium-high heat. Add your mix-ins (see opposite) and give them a quick sear, moving and scraping with a spatula as needed, until everything is cooked or heated through.

Add Your (Precooked) Noodles

You don't really need to fry or char the noodles (see opposite) for this recipe, so just get them in the wok, loosen them up, and make sure they're warmed through.

Sauce and Toss

Add the sauce and toss over the heat until everything is sticky and coated, 1 to 2 minutes. Serve with your choice of toppings (see opposite) and enjoy!

The key to this recipe is the sauce. Wok noodle sauce is a flavor bomb made up of umami-rich oyster, hoisin, and soy sauces mixed with rice vinegar and sugar. It's so addictive that we always keep a batch in a squeeze bottle in the fridge. It's the ultimate when you're fiending for a midnight noodle snack. Just prep some noodles, squeeze on some sauce, toss, and everything is right with the world. Follow the formula here to make the best wok noodles you'll ever taste.

Pick a Noodle

Wok noodle dishes typically call for fresh cooked oil noodles, which you can find in the refrigerated section of your local Asian grocery store. These noodles are perfectly chewy, and already cooked, so they only need a quick soak in warm water to loosen them up. You can also use lo mein, instant ramen, or even spaghetti in a pinch; just cook them according to the package directions and drain well.

Try: oil noodles, chow mein, wide rice noodles, rice vermicelli, macaroni

Pick Your Mix-Ins

When it comes to mix-ins like meat and veg, you can keep things simple, go over the top, or skip them altogether; we do all three on the regular. When we're feeling flush, we almost always do a combination of meat and seafood. No matter what mix-ins you choose, make sure everything is cut into bite-size pieces so it cooks quickly and at roughly the same rate.

Try: Chinese BBQ Pork (aka char siu; page 131), chicken thighs, steak, pork shoulder, any kind of sausage, ground meat, shrimp, squid, scallops, tofu puffs, vegetables, hearty leafy greens

Don't Skimp on the Toppings

Toppings are where it's at—they add visual interest, texture, flavors, and fun.

Try: Egg Ribbons (page 157), sliced green onions, chopped fresh cilantro, crispy fried onions (see page 239), mung bean sprouts, sliced raw shallots, lime wedges, fresh chilies

THE ESSENTIAL HOMEMADE

char siu

AKA CHINESE BBQ PORK

Nothing beats the unique savory flavor and char of char siu. Serve this as a topping for Wok Noodles (page 128), wonton noodle soup (page 166), or anything else you feel needs a bit of extra pork-y love.

The iconic red hue of char siu comes from tofu fermented with red rice *koji*. Like all fermented foods, it has a flavor and umami all its own. Look for jars of tofu cubes suspended in ruby-red liquid—they should be available at your local Asian grocery store or online. The tofu adds umami, salt, and, of course, color to this marinade.

The cut of pork is paramount to this dish. Some people prefer their char siu lean; others like it decadent and luxurious (i.e., fattier). We favor pork shoulder, which has a good ratio of fat marbling to meat. Pork belly is, of course, very rich, and if you can get your hands on pork jowl or cheek, it might just be the best cut of all.

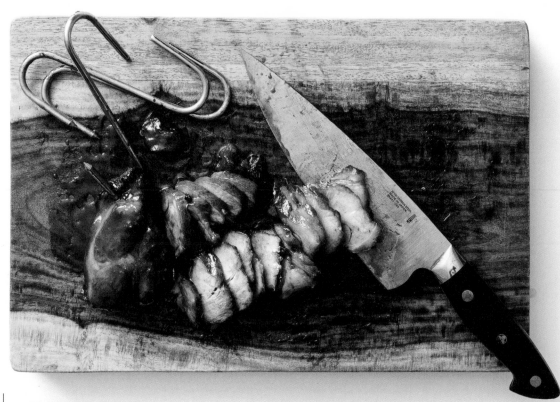

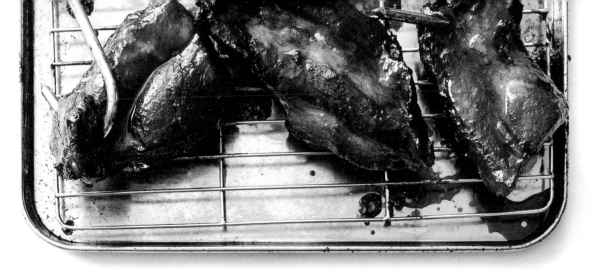

char Siu

Chinese BBQ Pork

1 cube red fermented tofu, with 1 tablespoon of its liquid

¼ cup honey

2 tablespoons hoisin sauce

1 tablespoon soy sauce

2 teaspoons Shaoxing wine (see page 235)

2 cloves garlic, peeled and smashed

1-inch piece fresh ginger, peeled and sliced

¼ teaspoon Chinese five-spice powder

¼ teaspoon ground white pepper

1 pound boneless pork shoulder (or the cut of your choice; see opposite)

1. Mash the red tofu with the tofu liquid in a large bowl. Add 2 tablespoons of the honey, along with the hoisin, soy sauce, Shaoxing wine, garlic, ginger, five-spice powder, and white pepper, and stir to combine. Add the pork and turn it to coat evenly with the marinade. Marinate, covered, in the fridge for a minimum of 12 hours and up to 24 hours.

2. Preheat your oven to 300°F. Line a rimmed baking sheet with aluminum foil and set a wire rack on top.

3. Remove the pork from the refrigerator and brush off the marinade, reserving the excess. Place the pork on the wire rack and roast, flipping halfway through, for 1 hour.

4. Meanwhile, make the glaze: Remove the ginger and garlic from the marinade and pour the marinade into a small saucepan. Stir in the remaining 2 tablespoons of honey and bring to a boil over medium-low heat. When the glaze has reduced a little and can coat the back of a spoon, 3 to 4 minutes, remove it from the heat and set aside.

5. When the pork has roasted for an hour, increase the oven temperature to 400°F. Brush the char siu with the honey glaze and roast, until glistening and slightly charred on the edges, 2 to 5 minutes. Flip with tongs, brush again, and roast for another 2 to 3 minutes. Remove from the oven and let rest for 5 minutes. Cut pieces diagonally into ¼- to ½-inch-thick slices and enjoy.

Makes about 1 pound

Make It Ahead

To make the char siu ahead of time, let the roasted pork cool completely, unsliced, then store it in an airtight container in the fridge. It will keep for 3 to 4 days.

5

SOUP-ER NOODLES TO THE RESCUE

NOODLES TO SOOTHE YOUR SOUL

A great bowl of noodle soup heals your soul.

Often when people hear "noodles," they think of soup noodles, and that's partly because soup noodles are some of the greatest food that humanity has ever developed. What other dish can be so simultaneously comforting, filling, warm, simple yet complex, and humble yet sophisticated? The broths that make soup noodles truly special sit up there with anything you might find in a fine dining restaurant. And even the most accessible, affordable bowls (if done right) are beautifully composed and perfectly balanced. Soup noodles are democratic: It doesn't matter how much money you have; the best soup noodles are affordable to almost anyone. Good soup takes time, and we can't get around that, but the recipes in this chapter are all worthy of your time. After all, waiting while your house fills with delicious smells is part of the experience of making a perfect noodle soup.

HELLO
my name is

Pho

Pho hasn't been around that long—only about 100 years—but in its short life it's been beloved, controversial, hotly debated, and made and remade far and wide. There's no right or wrong way to make pho. Even in Vietnam there are disagreements about origins, ingredients, and methods. The secret to great pho is to season fearlessly, knowing that it will all work out at the end. You want a sweet, slightly overseasoned broth that will be balanced once the noodles are added and it's hit with a fresh squeeze of lime. This takes experience and a willingness to go a little too far with the fish sauce or salt, but if you set some unseasoned broth aside, you can always fix any mistakes and really figure out how to dial in your perfect pho, risk free.

Pho is about balance, and besides being delicious, the toppings in pho are meant to complement each other texturally. The house special in most pho restaurants gives you many different cuts of meat for a reason: It's so much better that way. When you're feeling especially adventurous, try to find as many cuts of beef as you can and see if you enjoy the contrasting flavors and textures.

1 Sirloin

Thinly sliced sirloin is probably the easiest thing to find, and the most familiar, too. Look for a sirloin roast and see if the shop will slice it for you; if not, freeze it a little to make it easier to cut those signature super-thin slices.

2 Flank and Brisket

Flank and brisket are forgiving slow-cooking cuts that should be simmered with the broth for at least an hour, then chilled before being sliced. Properly cooked, the meat will be well done and melt-in-your-mouth tender, with a strong pho flavor.

3 Meatballs

Vietnamese beef meatballs are super dense and chewy in the best way. You can usually find them at an Asian supermarket. These meatballs come precooked, so all you need to do is slice them in half and drop them into boiling water (we drop them into the same pot as the pho noodles) for a minute to heat them up.

4 Omasum

Omasum is a kind of tripe, sometimes called bible tripe. It can seem scary when you first buy it, but it's crunchy and delicious. It should look extremely white and hopefully will come pre-sliced. This is not a cut you'll find at a supermarket, but any Asian grocery store with a meat department will carry it. As with the meatballs, just drop it in boiling water for a minute to prepare.

5 Tendon

Of all the beef cuts described here, tendon is probably the hardest to get, but also by far the most rewarding. You'll probably need to ask for it from a butcher, then cut it down into bite-size pieces. Boil the tendon with the broth for about 2 hours to get it to that addictive, slightly crunchy yet melt-in-your-mouth consistency that so many pho lovers crave.

6 Onions and Cilantro

Sliced sweet onions and green onions and chopped fresh cilantro add a huge hit of brightness and freshness to your broth. We like to slice both kinds of onions super thin and drop them into the pho along with the cilantro just before serving.

7 Bean Sprouts, Jalapeño, and Lime

Mung bean sprouts add crunch and subtle flavor to your broth. Some people enjoy them and some don't, so bean sprouts are typically served on a side plate for you to add as desired. You can serve them raw or briefly blanched. Thinly sliced jalapeños and wedges of limes are added to the bean sprouts plate. The jalapeño is optional, but the lime is highly recommended. We like to add our lime halfway through the bowl to change the taste of the pho mid-meal.

8 Thai Basil

Thai basil doesn't taste much like the usual sweet basil that's everywhere; it's sharper and more floral. You can find it in a clamshell in the herbs section of most good supermarkets.

Regarding Hoisin and Sriracha
A chef was famously criticized for demanding that his diners forgo these sauces to maintain the purity of his pho. We don't necessarily agree, but either way, hoisin and sriracha make great dips for the meat on the side.

This is our best version of the classic beef pho the world has come to know and love. We use roasted beef marrow bones to infuse this pho with richness far beyond its cooking time. You'll need to watch the broth and make sure it doesn't cook down too much; look to end up with about 4 cups of liquid. We double strain all of our soups for the best slurping experience: once as it comes out of the pot to catch large pieces, and again as it goes in the bowl to catch the fine bits. Because not everyone has a giant stockpot, this recipe was written to serve two people, but if you have a larger pot, you can definitely double or triple this recipe without much extra effort. Like fine wine or whiskey, a good noodle soup needs a good bowl. A high-sided bowl that can hold 3 to 4 cups of liquid is perfect (see page xv), but in a pinch, you could even use a mixing bowl.

THE HOUSE SPECIAL

ROASTED BONE MARROW AND BEEF BRISKET PHO

2 beef marrow bones (each about 2 inches long)

1-inch piece fresh ginger, halved lengthwise

1 medium yellow onion, peeled and halved

½ pound beef brisket, fat trimmed

1 cinnamon stick

1 teaspoon whole cloves

2 star anise pods

5 to 6 cardamom pods (optional)

1 teaspoon coriander seeds (optional)

1 teaspoon fennel seeds (optional)

3 tablespoons fish sauce, or to taste

2 tablespoons sugar, or to taste

6 ounces dried pho noodles

Fresh Thai basil, mung bean sprouts, lime wedges, sliced jalapeño, and sliced green onion (see page 138), for serving

1. Preheat your oven to 450°F.

2. Arrange the marrow bones, ginger, and one onion half, cut side up, in a baking dish. Roast until the bones are dry and browned and the top of the onion is charred, about 40 minutes.

3. Meanwhile, place the brisket in a large pot, add water to cover (about 5 cups), and bring to a rolling boil over high heat. Let cook for 15 minutes, then reduce to a simmer. Skim the surface with a spoon, discarding any scum that has accumulated.

4. When the marrow bones and aromatics are done, remove them from the baking dish and add them to the stock, along with any accumulated juices in the dish.

5. Toast the cinnamon stick, cloves, star anise, and all the other spices, if using, in a small dry baking dish in the still-hot oven for 2 to 3 minutes, then add them to the stock as well. (Alternatively, toast them in a small dry pan on the stovetop over medium-low heat.) Continue simmering the stock for 1 more hour. The brisket will be tender but not falling apart.

6. Carefully transfer the brisket to a bowl or high-sided pan. Cover and refrigerate it until you are ready to use it.

Serves 2

5x Better

Don't just stop at brisket; add some of the other meats listed on page 138. Add them to the broth along with the sliced brisket in Step 8.

Make It Ahead

The stock can be made ahead of time, then cooled and stored, covered, in the refrigerator for 3 to 4 days. When you are ready to serve, transfer it to a medium pot and jump right into Step 8.

Continued on next page ⟶

7. Top up the stock with water to equal about 4 cups. Season with fish sauce and sugar to taste, adding each a tablespoon at a time until the stock tastes just on the verge of being overseasoned. Strain the stock through a mesh strainer if you'd like, or use a slotted spoon to remove the large aromatics and bones. Spoon out any remaining marrow in the bones and add it to the broth, or eat it (chef's treat). At this point, if you are making the broth ahead of time, let it cool completely, then cover and refrigerate.

8. When you are almost ready to serve, bring the stock back up to a simmer over medium-high heat. At the same time, bring a medium pot of water to a boil over high heat. Slice the brisket against the grain into $\frac{1}{8}$-inch slices and add it to the stock to warm up. Thinly slice the remaining raw onion half and set it aside.

9. Add the noodles to the boiling water and cook according to the package directions. Drain well, then divide the noodles between two warmed bowls.

10. Ladle 2 cups of piping-hot broth through a fine-mesh strainer into each bowl. Slightly loosen the noodles with a pair of chopsticks, then top with the sliced brisket, yellow and green onion, and cilantro. Serve immediately, with a big plate of Thai basil, bean sprouts, lime wedges, and sliced jalapeño alongside.

Taiwanese beef noodle soup has a cult following. It's the soul food of Taiwan and the absolute first thing you should eat when landing in Taipei. Taiwanese beef noodle soup has a deep, dark flavor so complex and layered that you'll keep eating it after you're full, trying to figure out what makes it so good. The secrets to this savory, slightly spicy bowl of noodles are a toasted spice mix, deeply seared and caramelized aromatics, and a triple whammy of tomato, doubanjiang (chili bean paste), and soy sauce. Taiwanese beef noodle soup doesn't have as much popular buzz as ramen or pho, but it's Taiwan's pride and joy for a reason—it's packed with umami.

THE CULT CLASSIC

SUPER SAVORY TAIWANESE BEEF NOODLE SOUP

2 tablespoons neutral oil, plus more as needed

4 bone-in beef short ribs (about 2 pounds total)

2 tablespoons doubanjiang (see page 237)

½ medium onion, peeled and roughly chopped

3 green onions, cut into 3-inch pieces

2-inch piece fresh ginger, peeled and sliced

6 cloves garlic, peeled and crushed

1 hothouse tomato, quartered

2 tablespoons tomato paste

1 tablespoon sugar

¼ cup light soy sauce (see Note)

2 tablespoons Shaoxing wine (see page 235)

2 quarts sodium-free beef broth

1 cinnamon stick

Toasted Spice Mix (page 145)

24 ounces fresh ramen or Chinese oil noodles

4 to 8 stalks baby bok choy

1. Heat the 2 tablespoons of oil in a large Dutch oven over medium-high heat. Add the beef ribs and cook, turning occasionally, until deeply brown on all sides, 10 to 15 minutes. (Work in batches to avoid crowding the pan, adding oil as needed.) Transfer the beef ribs to a bowl, then reduce the heat to medium. Add the doubanjiang to the pan and cook, stirring, for 1 minute. Add the onion, green onions, and ginger and cook, without stirring, until caramelized, 3 to 5 minutes. Stir in the garlic, tomato, tomato paste, and sugar, continuing to brown until the sugar dissolves and the tomato starts to break down, 2 to 3 minutes.

2. Return the ribs to the Dutch oven (along with any juices that have collected in the bowl) and add the light soy sauce, Shaoxing wine, beef broth, cinnamon stick, and spice mix. Bring to a boil over medium-high heat, then reduce the heat to low and simmer, covered, until the ribs are extremely tender, about 2½ hours (add water as needed to maintain the volume of liquid). Transfer the ribs to a bowl and set aside.

3. Fill a large bowl with hot tap water and add the noodles. Let them loosen and warm through, 1 to 2 minutes. Drain well. Quickly blanch the bok choy in the hot soup.

Continued on page 145 ⟶

Serves 4

Toppings

Chili oil (preferably homemade, see page 53)
Sliced green onion
Chopped fresh cilantro

tip!

If you want an even more authentic bowl of noodles, buy some Chinese pickled mustard greens—get the ones that come in little foil pouches—and garnish to taste.

4. Ladle the piping-hot broth through a fine-mesh strainer into four warmed serving bowls, adding 2 cups of broth per bowl. Divide the noodles, bok choy, and ribs among the bowls. Serve immediately.

Note: The soy sauce that you choose to season the stock is of the ultimate importance. All soy sauces have a different salt content, so taste and season as you go, starting with a small amount and adding more gradually. Remember, you want your stock to be just a little too salty—the noodles and vegetables will soak up the flavor.

When making a stock with a bunch of spices, we like popping them into a giant disposable tea bag or a stainless steel tea infuser (both are very affordable online). You can also go the traditional route and wrap everything up in cheesecloth. Whichever method you choose, it will keep all the small bits together, making it easier to remove them from the stock.

Toasted Spice Mix

3 star anise pods

1 bay leaf

1 tablespoon fennel seeds

1 tablespoon cumin seeds

1 teaspoon Sichuan peppercorns

1 teaspoon coriander seeds

½ teaspoon whole cloves

Lightly toast the spices in a small dry pan over medium heat, shaking occasionally, until fragrant, 1 to 2 minutes. Remove from the heat and pop everything into a big tea bag. Set aside until ready to use.

Makes ¼ cup

This chicken pho is the easy weeknight version of our House Special pho (page 141). It cheats a little by using sodium-free chicken stock instead of water for an extra chicken-y boost. If you have the time and inclination to make your own chicken stock (see our 5X Better, below), you will absolutely be rewarded with a deeper, more flavorful pho, but this recipe is amazing even with store-bought stock because the real flavor is in the toasted spices and aromatics.

I FEEL LIKE CHICKEN TONIGHT

ULTIMATE WEEKNIGHT CHICKEN PHO

Serves 4

5x Better

If you want to go the extra distance, make your own stock: Place a whole chicken in a large ovenproof stockpot, add at least 8 cups of water (enough to cover the chicken completely), put on a lid, and cook in a 200°F oven for 6 to 8 hours. The result? An out-of-this-world chicken stock for this pho (or any other purpose). You can even remove the meat from the bones after you are done and use the meat for your pho so nothing is wasted. Although the chicken may be less flavorful than usual, its nothing a little hoisin or sriracha dip won't fix.

2 star anise pods

1 cinnamon stick

¼ teaspoon whole cloves

¼ teaspoon coriander seeds

¼ teaspoon fennel seeds (optional)

3 cardamom pods (optional)

2-inch piece fresh ginger, halved lengthwise

1 large onion, unpeeled, quartered

8 boneless, skin-on chicken breasts

2 quarts sodium-free chicken stock

About ¼ cup sugar

About ¼ cup fish sauce

12 ounces dried pho noodles

Fresh Thai basil, mung bean sprouts, sliced jalapeños, sliced green onion, and lime wedges (see page 138), for serving

1. In a dry, hot cast-iron pan over high heat, toast the star anise, cinnamon stick, cloves, coriander seeds, fennel seeds, and cardamom pods, if using, until fragrant, about 2 minutes. Remove the spices and set aside, then add the ginger and onion to the pan, cut sides down, and char, 3 to 4 minutes.

2. Combine the chicken breasts, chicken stock, and charred spices and aromatics in a large stockpot over high heat and bring to a boil. Reduce the heat to low and simmer, partially covered, for 1 hour. Add water as necessary to maintain the same amount of liquid as you started with.

3. Transfer the chicken to a bowl and refrigerate. Meanwhile, strain the stock through a mesh strainer or use a slotted spoon to remove as many solids as possible. Season the stock aggressively with sugar and fish sauce, a tablespoon of each at a time, until it's on the verge of being overseasoned.

4. When you are almost ready to serve, bring a medium pot of water to a boil over high heat. While the water comes to a boil, remove the chicken from the refrigerator and cut it into ½-inch-thick slices. Set it aside. Add the noodles to the boiling water and cook according to the package directions. Drain well.

5. Divide the noodles among four warmed bowls and bring the stock back up to a simmer in a clean pot. Add 2 cups of stock to each bowl, then top with the sliced chicken. Serve immediately, with a big plate of Thai basil, bean sprouts, sliced jalapeños, sliced green onion, and lime wedges alongside.

tip!

If you own a pressure cooker, use it on high pressure for Step 2 and you'll reduce the simmer time from 1 hour to 10 minutes.

HELLO
my name is

Laksa

At its heart, laksa is about the play between savory stock, noodles, and toppings. It's a glorious mess of flavors and textures: everything you could want in a bowl of noodles. Laksa hails from Malaysia, Singapore, and Indonesia, and there are as many regional types as there are types of ramen. But, unlike ramen with its instant appeal, laksa is still finding its way onto the international food scene. Still, those in the know know that laksa is an experience worth seeking out. Once you have your first bowl, you're going to crave another: rice noodles swimming in a rich and spicy coconut broth, seasoned with lemongrass, dried shrimp, chilies, and turmeric, and finished with cooked meats, seafoods, and fresh herbs. The vibrant yellow ocher broth packs huge umami flavor, with hints of sweet, sour, and savory. It's perfectly balanced with the noodles and toppings, creating a bowl with heft, texture, and undeniable deliciousness. Read on to dive deep into the world of laksa.

A good bowl of laksa is as much about the toppings as it is about the broth. The toppings should strike a balance between textures and flavors: crunchy, chewy, slippery, hearty, and light. Feel free to pile on the toppings, or keep your laksa simple with just noodles and broth. It's your choice. Here's what goes into a quality bowl of laksa:

1 Laksa Broth

The broth, or gravy, as it's called in Malaysia and Singapore, is an aromatic combination of chicken stock, shrimp stock, coconut milk, knotted pandan leaves (see below), and spicy complex laksa paste (see pages 152–155).

2 Pandan Leaves

You can find pandan leaves fresh or frozen at most Asian grocery stores. The shiny deep-green leaves impart a sweet and bright fragrance that hints at coconut. Knotted and simmered in the laksa stock, they'll add an extra bit of vibrancy and aroma.

3 Noodles

There's no right or wrong noodle to use in laksa. Sometimes people even mix noodles. We almost always use a thick vermicelli, but also common is thin vermicelli, or even yellow egg noodles.

4 Shredded Chicken and Shrimp

Since the base stock of laksa is made from chicken and shrimp stock, it only makes sense that chicken and shrimp are used as toppings. Typically, the chicken and shrimp are gently poached in water and the resulting light stock is used as the base for the soup.

5 Tofu Puffs

Most people would agree that tofu puffs are essential to any "real" bowl of laksa. The little deep-fried puffs—found in the tofu section at any Asian grocery store—soak up laksa broth like a sponge and absorb all of the flavors while they simmer.

6 Fish Balls

Fish balls, much like the tofu puffs, are simmered in the laksa broth. The idea is the same: a vehicle for absorbing laksa flavor. Pick them up in the frozen aisle at the Asian grocery store. There are a bunch of different kinds made of different types of seafood, but we prefer the golden (deep-fried) or classic white fish balls.

7 Eggs

Even before the put-an-egg-on-it phenomenon, eggs were a popular topping for laksa. Our all-time favorite is simple Egg Ribbons (page 157). They're bright yellow, mimicking noodles, and they swirl into the stock wonderfully.

8 Extras

Bean sprouts, smashed cucumber, sliced green onions, and fresh cilantro add crunch and freshness. A squeeze of lime adds acidity and balance.

Making your own laksa paste from scratch is intense.

In fact, most people, even in Southeast Asia, just go ahead and buy the paste at the store. Were you to do it from scratch, though, the results would be immensely rewarding. Homemade laksa paste is spicier, fresher, more satisfying (because you made it), and better tasting because you know exactly what's in it.

Every good laksa starts with a good laksa paste, made up of an abundance of aromatics, chilies, herbs, and dried shrimp, then cooked low and slow to caramelize and deepen the flavors. Even just gathering up the ingredients will take you a while, so it might be a good idea to double up on the paste recipe. You can freeze it and use it at a later date without any loss of flavor. A few tips: You might be tempted to speed up the cooking process, but as with caramelizing onions, a slow approach works best. You want the water content of the paste to cook out so you're left with an intense, condensed aromatic paste. At first the paste will be a vibrant yellow; at the end, you want it to be a deep chestnut brown. Finally, fry the paste outdoors if you can—the aromas can be overpowering in an enclosed or small space.

If you want to try it, here is a primer on the ingredients you'll need. (If you want laksa without the time investment, never fear—you can buy premade paste online. Our favorite is Prima Taste, but any paste from Southeast Asia is likely to do right by you.)

1 Dried Shrimp

Dried shrimp lend a sweet umami flavor to laksa (and other dishes). You'll probably have to make a special trip to an Asian grocery store to find them, or else order them online. When buying, look for them in the refrigerated section of any large Asian grocery store. Look for small clear bags of light pink, plump, oily, not-too-dry shrimp. Price increases as size increases, but you don't need to go for large shrimp here since you're going to blitz them in a food processor. Store dried shrimp in the freezer to preserve their freshness.

2 Dried Chilies and Fresh Chilies

The combination of fresh and dried chilies gives this laksa a mix of spice flavors, both bright and smoky. Fresh chilies give a bright pop of heat that contrasts nicely with the slow burn of dried. We like whole dried Sichuan Facing Heaven chilies, which are deep red and medium hot, but any small, medium-hot dried red chili will work here. If you're looking for a laksa with less heat, seed the fresh and dried chilies (for the dried, a quick pinch of the stem and shake of the chili will get most of the seeds out).

3 Fresh Galangal

Galangal makes up the bulk of laksa paste and it's what gives it that fresh, sharp, citrusy, lightly floral, almost piney flavor. Unfortunately, it's not something that can be easily substituted. You can buy it fresh at larger Asian grocery stores and sometimes they'll have it peeled, chopped, and frozen, which is next best.

4 Fresh Turmeric

You can find fresh turmeric, a root that looks a little like ginger, in most fancy-ish or organic grocery stores. Like its dried counterpart, fresh turmeric is a bright, intense orange-yellow. Be sure to cover your cutting board with plastic wrap and wear gloves when peeling it, otherwise you'll be spending some time scrubbing orange hands and surfaces.

5 Macadamia Nuts

We use roasted unsalted macadamia nuts to thicken our laksa paste. Although candlenuts are traditionally used in Southeast Asian cuisine, macadamia nuts are easier to come by and add a similar fat content and mouthfeel.

6 Belacan

Belacan is a block of hardened shrimp paste, and possibly the funkiest, most pungent ingredient that you will ever use. It is utterly essential to an authentic laksa. Made up of shrimp that is fermented, ground up, dried, and fermented again, belacan is incredibly powerful, in both smell and flavor, and adds a deep intense umami. Traditionally, it's toasted over low heat to coax out even more flavor. Try not to work with it indoors as the smell has a tendency to take over the room and linger. Belacan can be found at most Asian grocery stores and online.

LAKSA PASTE

Makes enough for 8 bowls

This is one of those recipes that just might have you running all over town, cursing the fact that you need weird, esoteric ingredients you'll probably never use again. But stay with us here—it's well worth the treasure hunt. The result is an incredibly aromatic paste, kind of like a magical umami booster.

About ½ cup (2¼ ounces) dried shrimp

4 to 8 dried red Sichuan chilies, stemmed

3½ ounces galangal, peeled and chopped (about 1 cup)

1 tablespoon chopped fresh turmeric (about ⅓ ounce)

1 cup chopped shallots

1 head garlic, cloves separated and peeled

2 or 3 large fresh Fresno or other red chilies, stemmed, seeded, and chopped

5 macadamia nuts (preferably roasted unsalted)

¼ cup (about 1½ ounces) belacan

4 stalks lemongrass, chopped (about 1 cup)

½ cup neutral oil

1. Soak the dried shrimp in 1 cup of warm water for 10 minutes. Drain well. Transfer the shrimp to the bowl of a food processor and process until finely chopped. Transfer the chopped shrimp to a bowl and set aside.

2. Place the dried chilies in a small bowl and add hot water to cover. Soak until soft, 10 minutes. Drain well.

3. Working in batches if needed, combine the galangal, turmeric, shallots, garlic, soaked and fresh chilies, macadamia nuts, belacan, and lemongrass in the bowl of the food processor (no need to clean it first) or a blender and process until everything is broken down into sandy, coarse crumbs.

4. Pour the oil into a large Dutch oven and add the galangal mixture, stirring to coat it evenly in oil. Fry over medium heat, stirring occasionally, until the paste becomes fragrant, 15 to 20 minutes.

5. Add the chopped dried shrimp to the Dutch oven and cook, stirring, until the paste becomes a deep, caramelized brown, 5 to 10 minutes. At this point, you can use the paste to make laksa stock, or you can let it cool completely, transfer it to an airtight container, and store with plastic wrap pressed against the surface of the paste (it will keep in the fridge for up to 1 week, and in the freezer for up to 2 months).

tip!

If you prep it in advance and freeze it, a heady bowl of laksa will never be too far away. We use this flavorful paste in other ways too, not just as the base of laksa: Toss hot pasta with a bit of laksa paste and pasta water and boom, instant deliciousness. Before freezing the laksa paste, divide it into ½-cup portions so you can make one bowl of laksa at a time.

EGG RIBBONS

THE LESSER KNOWN EGG NOODLE

It's always fun when food dresses up as other food—say, a bright pile of yellow noodles that aren't noodles? Egg ribbons are a quick and easy way to add color and protein. They look impressive and are incredibly easy to make. Make sure you use a nonstick pan and keep the heat on the lower side; you don't want your brilliant yellow eggs browning too much.

Egg Ribbons

1 large egg

Pinch of salt

Neutral oil, for the pan

Makes 1 portion, but infinitely scalable

1. Lightly beat the egg in a bowl until completely incorporated. Season with salt.

2. Heat a medium (12-inch) nonstick frying pan on medium-low heat. Add a touch of oil to the pan and swirl to coat.

3. Pour the egg into the pan in a thin layer and swirl to coat the bottom of the pan, much like a crepe. Cook, untouched, over low heat until the egg sets and releases from the side of the pan, about 1 minute. Use a silicone spatula to flip the egg and cook the other side, 10 to 15 seconds.

4. Slide the egg onto a cutting board. Carefully roll it up and thinly slice crosswise into ribbons. Use immediately, or cover and keep in the fridge for up to 3 days.

tip!

When making multiple portions, stack several crepes at a time before rolling and slicing them to cut down on the work.

Making laksa broth can be as simple as combining the laksa paste with chicken stock and coconut milk, but we punch it up a bit by poaching chicken (which will later be shredded and used as a topping) in chicken stock instead of water. Shrimp shells add a sweet brininess, and knotted pandan leaves add an aromatic tropical flavor. Most laksa broths are purposely left with bits of paste mingling with the stock, which gives them a slightly sandy texture, but we prefer a smooth, rich broth, so we usually strain out the solids. You can feel free to strain out the laksa paste or leave it in; the soup will be amazing either way.

KING OF NOODLES

LAKSA: THE OTHER NOODLE SOUP YOU NEVER KNEW YOU LOVED

1 pound boneless, skinless chicken breasts

Salt

3 cups sodium-free chicken stock

1 pound large shell-on shrimp, peeled and deveined, and shells reserved

2 pandan leaves, knotted together

2 cups laksa paste (preferably homemade; see page 155)

3 cans (14 ounces each) full-fat coconut milk (see Notes)

1 tablespoon sugar, or to taste

1 package (6 ounces) fish balls

1 package (4 ounces) tofu puffs

12 ounces dried rice vermicelli (see Notes)

4 portions Egg Ribbons (page 157)

1. Generously season the chicken with salt. Place it in a stockpot and add the stock, reserved shrimp shells, and pandan leaves. Bring to a boil over medium-high heat, skimming off any foam. Reduce the heat to low and let simmer, covered, until the chicken is cooked through (cut a piece open to test it), 8 to 12 minutes. Use tongs to carefully remove the chicken from the stock. Let the chicken cool, then shred the meat and set aside.

2. Use a strainer to remove and discard the shrimp shells and pandan leaves. Stir in the laksa paste and coconut milk and bring the mixture back up to a simmer. Add the sugar and 2 teaspoons of salt to the broth; taste and adjust each as needed.

3. Add the shrimp to the laksa broth and continue to simmer until the shrimp are pink and cooked through, 2 to 3 minutes. Scoop the shrimp out with a strainer and set aside. Add the fish balls and tofu puffs and keep the broth at a low simmer, partially covered.

4. Bring a large pot of water to a boil over high heat. Cook the noodles according to the package directions and drain well.

5. Ladle 2 cups of the broth through a strainer into each of four warmed bowls. Divide the noodles among the bowls, and top each with some of the shredded chicken, fish balls, tofu puffs, shrimp, and egg ribbons. Serve immediately.

Serves 4

Toppings

Mung bean sprouts
Cucumber matchsticks
Sliced green onions
Fresh cilantro leaves
Lime wedges

Notes: Opt for a full-fat coconut milk without stabilizers. Our favorite is Aroy-D. It's thick, creamy, and pure.

Laksa can contain ordinary thin rice vermicelli, thick vermicelli similar to what we use in Bun Bo Hue (page 81), or Chinese egg noodles. Occasionally it is even served with a mix of rice and wheat noodles (although we are actually horrified by this—only do this if you also mix your cereals, you monster). Feel free to use your noodle of choice.

 tip! This broth is infinitely scalable—feel free to double or triple the recipe as needed. If you're making one bowl of laksa, you need 1¼ cups coconut milk, ¾ cup chicken stock, ½ cup laksa paste, half a knotted pandan leaf, ½ teaspoon sugar, and ¼ teaspoon salt.

Purists will say this isn't *technically* a laksa because it's vegan, but red curry paste, coconut milk, and Chinese sesame paste combine beautifully to create a spicy, creamy, nutty stock that's surprisingly close to the traditional dish. When you want laksa in a hurry, this is the recipe you'll turn to again and again.

You Can Have it All

ACCIDENTALLY VEGAN WEEKNIGHT LAKSA

Serves 4

Toppings

Mung bean sprouts
Cucumber matchsticks
Chopped fresh cilantro
Sliced green onions
Slice red onion
Lime wedges

tip!

Look for the Aroy-D brand of Thai red curry paste. It's our favorite.

1 tablespoon neutral oil

4 cloves garlic, peeled and smashed

1-inch piece fresh ginger, peeled and thinly sliced

4 tablespoons red curry paste

2 cans (14 ounces each) full-fat coconut milk

1 quart sodium-free vegetable stock

2 tablespoons Chinese sesame paste (see page 236)

2 stalks lemongrass, bruised

1 package (16 ounces) firm tofu, cut into ¾-inch cubes

1 package (4 ounces) tofu puffs

12 ounces dried rice vermicelli

1. Heat the oil in a stockpot over medium heat. Add the garlic and ginger and cook until fragrant, 1 minute.

2. Stir in the curry paste and fry until the oils start to separate from the solids, 2 to 3 minutes. Stir in the coconut milk, vegetable stock, sesame paste, and ½ cup cold water. Add the lemongrass. Turn the heat up to medium-high and bring the soup to a boil.

3. Add the tofu cubes and puffs, reduce the heat to low, and simmer until the tofu and tofu puffs are heated through and the flavors concentrate, 10 to 15 minutes.

4. Meanwhile, bring a large pot of water to a boil over high heat. Add the vermicelli and cook according to the package directions. Drain well.

5. Ladle 2 cups of the broth through a strainer into each of four warmed bowls. Divide the noodles, tofu, and tofu puffs evenly among the bowls. Serve immediately.

WONTONS

ARE DEFINITELY A NOODLE

Are wontons a noodle? Most people would say no, but if you think about it, isn't a wonton just a tender little pork and shrimp meatball enclosed in a thin, noodle-like wrapper? Doesn't that mean wontons are just stuffed noodles, much like ravioli or tortellini? Those are noodles, right? Okay, good—we're in agreement. Wontons are noodles.

And what glorious noodles they are. There's a huge variation in what people put in their wontons: chicken, fish, even tofu. We like a mix of pork and shrimp in ours—the fattiness of ground pork and the sweetness of shrimp play off each other wonderfully, both taste- and texture-wise.

Even though it's tempting, try not to overstuff wontons—they taste better when the skin-to-filling ratio is balanced. Speaking of the wonton skins, head on over to your local Asian grocery store and buy the square wrappers located in the fresh section, near the noodles. Round wrappers are usually for potstickers and other dumplings, so you want the squares—they're made of a thin egg dough.

PS: If you're in a hurry, you can buy frozen wontons at an Asian grocery store or at most supermarkets.

SHRIMP AND PORK WONTONS

½ pound shrimp, peeled and deveined

¼ cup dried sliced wood ear mushrooms, soaked in hot water for 10 minutes

½ pound ground pork

2 green onions, white parts only, thinly sliced

1 small shallot, peeled and diced

1 clove garlic, peeled and crushed

2 teaspoons light soy sauce, plus extra as needed

2 teaspoons Shaoxing wine (see page 235)

1 teaspoon toasted sesame oil

½ teaspoon freshly ground black pepper

12 ounces fresh wonton wrappers (about ½ package)

Spicy Sichuan Wonton Chili Sauce, for serving (optional—only if you're eating the wontons on their own; recipe follows)

1. Place the shrimp on a cutting board and use a sharp knife to roughly chop half of the shrimp and finely chop the rest. (You want some of it a bit chunky and some of it closer to a paste to give the filling a mixture of textures.) Transfer to a large bowl.

2. Drain the mushrooms and roughly chop them. Add the mushrooms to the shrimp in the bowl, then add the ground pork, green onions, shallot, garlic, soy sauce, Shaoxing wine, sesame oil, and pepper. (You may need to add more soy sauce—test it by microwaving a tiny patty of the meat mixture or frying it in oil and tasting.)

3. Set up a wonton wrapping station with a small bowl of water, the bowl of filling, the wonton wrappers covered with plastic wrap or a damp paper towel, and a plate or tray to put the finished wontons on.

4. Lay a wonton wrapper down diagonally on a work surface so that it looks like a diamond. Place 2 teaspoons of the filling in the middle. Dip your finger into the bowl of water and lightly run it along the edges of the wrapper. Fold the wrapper from the bottom corner to the top corner to create a triangle, using your fingers to seal the filling inside and push out any air bubbles. Wet the two side corners of the triangle and pull them together over the filling, pinching to close. Cover the finished wonton with a damp paper towel or plastic wrap (the wrappers have a tendency to dry out), and repeat with the remaining wrappers and filling. At this point, the wontons should be cooked or frozen (see Tip).

5. To cook the wontons, bring a large pot of water to a boil over medium-high heat. Add the wontons, stirring gently so they don't stick to the bottom of the pot or each other. When the water comes back to a boil and the wontons float to the top, they should be cooked through, 4 to 6 minutes. (Cut one open to check.) Drain well.

6. Use the wontons as directed in our Hong Kong Special (page 166) or the soup of your choice. If you're serving them on their own, place them in a large bowl and drizzle and toss with the chili sauce.

Makes 1 pound (enough for 2 to 4, or 1 Mike)

Toppings

Sliced green onions
Crispy fried shallots (see page 239)

tip!

If you can't cook the wontons immediately, freeze them—even if you plan on using them later the same day. This will avoid sad and soggy wontons with broken skins. Spread the uncooked wontons in a single layer 1 to 2 inches apart on a rimmed baking sheet and place them in the freezer. When they are frozen solid, transfer them to a freezer-safe airtight container or ziplock bag. To cook frozen wontons, add a couple of extra minutes to the cooking time. Extra wonton skins can be tightly wrapped in plastic wrap and frozen; defrost them completely before using.

Spicy Sichuan Wonton Chili Sauce

2 cloves garlic, peeled and minced

2 tablespoons chili oil (preferably homemade; see page 53), or to taste

2 tablespoons soy sauce

2 tablespoons toasted sesame oil

1 tablespoon Chinese black vinegar

2 tablespoons sliced green onions

1 tablespoon chopped fresh cilantro

Whisk together all of the ingredients in a small bowl to incorporate. Let the sauce stand until the flavors meld, at least 10 minutes (it will keep in an airtight jar in the fridge for up to 5 days).

Makes 1 cup

If you've ever been to Hong Kong, then you'll know that one of the greatest comfort foods ever is wonton noodle soup. This version is just as good, and maybe even better, because no pants required. You don't have to fly across the ocean (or even leave the house) for it. Lots of wonton soups are literally just wontons floating in chicken stock, but here we went the Hong Kong–inspired route and created a quick seafood stock from dried shrimp. The result is reminiscent of what you get in those tiny bowls on Wellington Street. If you have some pork fat on hand, add a teaspoon to each bowl for even more authenticity—it's the secret to the savory richness of the bowls you find in Hong Kong.

SHRIMP AND PORK WONTONS

WONTON NOODLE SOUP LIKE THEY DO IN HKG

Serves 4

Toppings

Chili oil (preferably
   homemade, see
   page 53)
Sliced green onions
Crispy fried shallots
   (see page 239)

8 cups sodium-free
   chicken stock

1-inch piece fresh ginger,
   peeled and sliced

2 cloves garlic, peeled
   and smashed

¼ cup dried shrimp (see
   page 153; optional but
   highly recommended)

4 tablespoons light soy
   sauce, or to taste

12 ounces fresh wonton
   egg noodles or chow
   mein noodles

1 pound Shrimp and Pork
   Wontons (page 163) or
   store-bought wontons
   (see Note)

4 to 8 stalks baby
   Chinese broccoli,
   trimmed

4 teaspoons toasted
   sesame oil

1. Combine the chicken stock, ginger, garlic, and dried shrimp, if using, in a stockpot over medium-low heat and bring to a gentle boil. Season with the soy sauce, starting with 2 tablespoons and adding more to taste—you want the broth to be just a touch too salty, which will flavor the noodles and Chinese broccoli. Reduce the heat to low and simmer, partially covered, while you prepare the rest of the soup.

2. Bring two large pots of water to a boil over high heat. Add the noodles to one pot and cook according to the package directions. Remove the noodles with tongs (reserve the boiling water) and place them in a colander, rinse in cold water, and drain well.

3. Meanwhile, in the other pot, add the wontons to the boiling water and cook, occasionally stirring gently to prevent the wontons from sticking to the bottom of the pot or each other. The wontons are cooked when they float to the top (cut one open to check), 4 to 6 minutes; remove them to a bowl with a slotted spoon. Add the Chinese broccoli to the boiling wonton water. Cook until slightly wilted, about 1 minute.

4. Divide the noodles and sesame oil among four warmed bowls. Ladle 2 cups of the stock into each bowl, then divide the wontons and Chinese broccoli among them. Serve immediately.

Note: Homemade wontons are always best, but you can find great frozen ones at most supermarkets and at Asian grocery stores. For this soup, try to find wontons filled with pork and shrimp.

We had an amazing bowl of Mexican soup with vermicelli at Chef Rick Bayless's excellent Xoco grill in Chicago many years ago and were so enamored of it that we re-created it right when we got back home. Over the years our version has changed so much that it doesn't really resemble the original anymore, but in our hearts it's still an homage to the Xoco version. It's the combination of the fresh and canned smoked peppers that forms the base of this soup's incredible flavor. If you don't have access to Fresno peppers or find them too spicy, you can substitute any red pepper, including red bell peppers; the roasting process is still the same.

SOUTHWEST RAMEN

WEEKNIGHT CHIPOTLE ADOBO PORK BELLY RAMEN

Serves 4

Toppings

Thinly sliced onion
Fresh cilantro leaves

5x Better

If you live the Southwest and it's the right season, switching out the red chiles for local greens (such as Hatch or Big Jim) will take this to a whole new level.

Try torching the chiles with a kitchen blowtorch instead of roasting them. It's a little more hands on, but you'll be rewarded with a far deeper, smokier flavor.

1 pound small nugget potatoes, halved

2 medium zucchinis, cut into 1-inch cubes

5 medium red Fresno chiles

2 tablespoons neutral oil

Salt

1 pound pork belly

1 can (7 ounces) chipotle chiles in adobo

Juice of 2 limes

2 tablespoons sugar

1 tablespoon soy sauce

2 cloves garlic, peeled and crushed

24 ounces fresh ramen noodles

2 quarts sodium-free beef stock

Baby arugula, for serving

1. Preheat your oven to 425°F. Line two rimmed baking sheets with aluminum foil. Place a wire rack on one of the baking sheets for the pork belly.

2. Combine the potatoes, zucchini, and Fresno chiles in a large bowl. Add 1 tablespoon of the oil and a pinch of salt and toss to coat, then spread in a single layer on the lined baking sheet. Rub the pork belly with the remaining 1 tablespoon of oil and season on both sides with salt. Place it on the wire rack. Roast the vegetables and pork belly in the oven until the pork belly is cooked through and tender, about 45 minutes, tossing the vegetables at the halfway mark.

3. Meanwhile, combine the chipotles and their sauce, the lime juice, 5 teaspoons of sugar, and the soy sauce in a blender and blend until smooth. Transfer to a small bowl and set aside. No need to wash the blender.

4. When the skin of the Fresno chiles has blackened and charred, about 25 minutes, remove them from the oven (return the remaining vegetables to the oven to continue roasting with the pork belly) and transfer to a ziplock bag. Seal the bag and allow the chiles to steam until their skins have loosened, about 10 minutes. Remove and discard the skins and stems (you may want to wear gloves to protect your hands), and transfer the chile flesh to the blender, along with the garlic, the remaining 1 teaspoon of sugar, 1 teaspoon of salt, and ½ cup of water. Blend until smooth, then transfer to a small bowl, cover, and set aside.

5. When the pork belly and vegetables are done, remove them from the oven and let rest. Bring a large pot of water to a boil over high heat. Add the noodles and cook

according to the package directions; drain well. Bring the beef stock to a simmer in a medium pot over low heat and hold. Slice the pork belly into ½-inch-thick slices.

6. Place 1 tablespoon of the chipotle mixture and 1 teaspoon of the Fresno mixture into each of four warmed bowls, then ladle 2 cups of beef broth into each. Divide the noodles among the bowls and top each with a few slices of the pork belly and some of the vegetables. Serve piping hot, with the arugula in a bowl and the remaining chipotle and Fresno mixtures alongside as condiments.

6

THE ULTIMATE NOODLE

LAYERS ON LAYERS OF LASAGNA

We love big noodles and we cannot lie.

If you think about it, lasagna is the ultimate noodle: It's big, it's wide, it's noodle heaven. Lasagna is literally the most giant noodle. When it's stacked up and layered with cheeses and sauce, it becomes the dish of the same name—and a noodle lover's dream. Because lasagna is an all-out kind of noodle, we've gone all out with our lasagna recipes. There are eight in total here, and in true #thatnoodlelife style, we pit them against each other in an epic lasagna bracket competition (page 176). It's a comfort noodle hunger games for the one lasagna to rule them all. Live long and lasagna 🖖.

Lasagna Pans

The recipes in this chapter make enough sauce to fill a standard 9 x 13-inch lasagna pan, but why be rectangular when you can be creative? Look around your kitchen: Any deep-ish baking dish is a contender for crispier cheese edges and unique nooks and crannies. You might end up with leftover noodles or sauce depending on what pan you use—but that's never a bad thing, it just makes for a quirkier, more genuine lasagna. In fact, you'll notice that in all of our photos we don't ever use a traditional lasagna pan, because where's the fun in that? Lasagna is all about that cozy noodle chill, though, so go with whatever's easiest—even if it's a disposable foil pan.

Seasoning

Remember to season your lasagna cooking water as well as the sauces. Lasagna is a big noodle and needs big flavor. For best results, sacrifice a bit of a noodle, top it with the sauces, add the necessary amount of cheese, and taste before committing to making the entire tray. Nothing is sadder than an underseasoned lasagna.

Noodles

We tested all of the recipes with store-bought dried noodles, store-bought fresh noodles, and homemade, using fresh double-yolk pasta dough (see page 13) rolled to thickness #5 instead of #4 and trimmed to fit. Homemade was the clear winner, of course, but for ease, our pick is store-bought fresh noodles. If you're using fresh noodles, either homemade or store-bought, you don't have to boil them before layering, which is a bonus.

Dried lasagna noodles should be cooked in a large pot of salted boiling water according to the package directions and then shocked in an ice water bath to prevent them from overcooking. Drain the noodles well— you don't want any water clinging to them. Separate the noodles, making sure none of them are sticking together, and lay them flat in a single layer on a lightly oiled rimmed baking sheet, plate, or cutting board. When it comes to store-bought dried noodles, go with curly edges or flat—we don't really have a preference.

Layering

Is a lasagna really a lasagna if it doesn't have at least three layers? We say no. We usually aim for four or more layers, with an emphasis on more (often opting for small-ish baking dishes to get more layer bang for our buck). When layering your lasagna, keep in mind the sauce-to-cheese-to-noodle ratio. Some people like lasagnas on the saucy side, and some like a little more structure. We've settled on about 1 cup of sauce plus a generous dusting of cheese for each layer (about as much as the first light dusting of snow of the year when you want the schools to be closed, but they aren't, and you have to console yourself by cuddling up with a warm hearty lasagna). As for the noodles, overlap them only slightly. You don't want any double noodle layers, but you also don't want spaces with just sauce. Trim the noodles if needed to fit just right; they should be flush against the sides of your pan.

Resting

One last thing: Lasagna tastes amazing the day it's made, but it's even better the next day, after the noodles and sauce have had a chance to meld into a delicious, cohesive dish. Whatever you do, don't forget to let your lasagna cool for at least 10 to 15 minutes after it comes out of the oven. Like a good steak, lasagna needs to rest: Not only will it slice more neatly, but the sauce and fillings will stay right where you want them—in between the layers.

Besciamella Sauce

Makes 4 cups

Many of our lasagnas are layered with a classic besciamella sauce, the Italian version of béchamel. The recipe is super simple and makes enough for one batch of lasagna.

4 tablespoons (½ stick) unsalted butter

6 tablespoons all-purpose flour

4 cups (1 quart) whole milk

1½ cups finely grated Parmigiano-Reggiano cheese

Salt

1. Melt the butter in a medium (at least 2-quart) saucepan over medium-low heat.

2. Sprinkle the flour onto the melted butter, whisking constantly until smooth and completely incorporated (if it starts to brown, reduce the heat to low), about 3 minutes.

3. Add the milk in a thin stream while whisking. The mixture might start out lumpy, but keep whisking and it will smooth out. Cook over medium heat, whisking occasionally, until the sauce comes to a simmer and reduces slightly to the consistency of thickened cream, about 10 minutes.

4. Remove the sauce from the heat and whisk in the Parmigiano. Taste and season with salt. Cover and keep warm on very low heat until you're ready to build your lasagna, or let it cool completely and store in the fridge, tightly covered, for up to 5 days.

tip!

Reheat refrigerated besciamella before using it: Warm it in a saucepan over very low heat, stirring to loosen. Add 2 tablespoons to ¼ cup of milk to help thin it if needed.

OUR BRACKET COMPETITION DREAM

We first toyed with the idea of a lasagna bracket competition years ago as a way to rank all the different lasagna recipes on the internet. We never made it past the first head-to-head. There are a number of different reasons—namely, the sheer cost and time (and tummy) commitment involved in making so many lasagnas became prohibitive. It took us a week to even finish eating the two lasagnas we had made.

But the lasagna bracket dream never died, and when we ~~needed~~ wanted to cook and shoot eight different lasagnas for this book, we knew it was fate. We conducted a double-blind tasting, judged each lasagna separately and then together, and came out with our ultimate ranking of these eight lasagnas. It should be said, though, that while this competition yielded relative winners and losers, every single competitor is extremely delicious. Each lasagna is a winner in its own right—otherwise it never would have made the cut.

How do you do a double-blind taste test?

One of us labeled the lasagna samples from A to H and wrote down what lasagna each letter corresponded to. Then the other one changed the letters randomly from one to eight and wrote down the letter that corresponded to each number. We invited a bunch of friends over, and after that, it was as simple as closing our eyes as we tasted each bite. No one knew which lasagna they were eating, only the sample number.

Which lasagna won?

Unsurprisingly—because let's be honest, when you think lasagna, you think meat and cheese and red sauce—our over-the-top version of classic Bolognese lasagna (see page 178) won the day among all the judges. Surprisingly, we both independently put the very untraditional (by American standards) chicken lasagna (see page 185) in second place. (We totally disregarded the other judges when it came to second-to-eighth places as they all wildly disagreed with each other.)

Should I conduct my own competition?

Yes, definitely. Some of those friends actually went home and did their own lasagna competitions. Some even accused their opponents of cheating by using store-bought sauces.

Reasonably, you can make all of the lasagnas in two to three days. The lasagnas with red meat sauces (Bolognese, Carnevale, and creamy pork sugo) take longer to make, just because most of the sauces have a minimum simmer time; you'll want to start on those first. You'll also need three batches of the Besciamella Sauce (page 175). If you're a confident cook, you can triple the recipe. It will become harder to control the lumps in your roux and how the sauce cooks and thickens, but it's not difficult. Or you can buy disposable half-size lasagna pans and only make half-sized lasagnas, which would require one and a half batches of the creamy sauce.

The good news is that you can make and store all of the sauces a few days in advance. It's far easier if you think of this as a make-ahead affair and have all of the sauces and components ready to go before you start assembling any lasagnas (or better yet, enlist some friends to help and assign a lasagna to each). Do yourself a favor and buy fresh lasagna sheets from the grocery store (you'll find them with the fresh ravioli and tortellini). The noodles are no-boil, so that will save you a step. Once everything is layered, the finished lasagnas can hang out in the fridge until all their lasagna friends are ready.

Once your lasagnas are assembled, they can all go in the oven and bake at the same time. The goal when baking is to amplify and meld the flavors, melt the cheese, and make sure that everything is heated through. When baking multiple lasagnas at once, be sure to rotate and switch the pans on the racks so everything gets an even bake. If you can't fit all eight in at the same time, bake them in two batches and allow the second batch to rest for at least 15 minutes before starting the competition.

Our Results

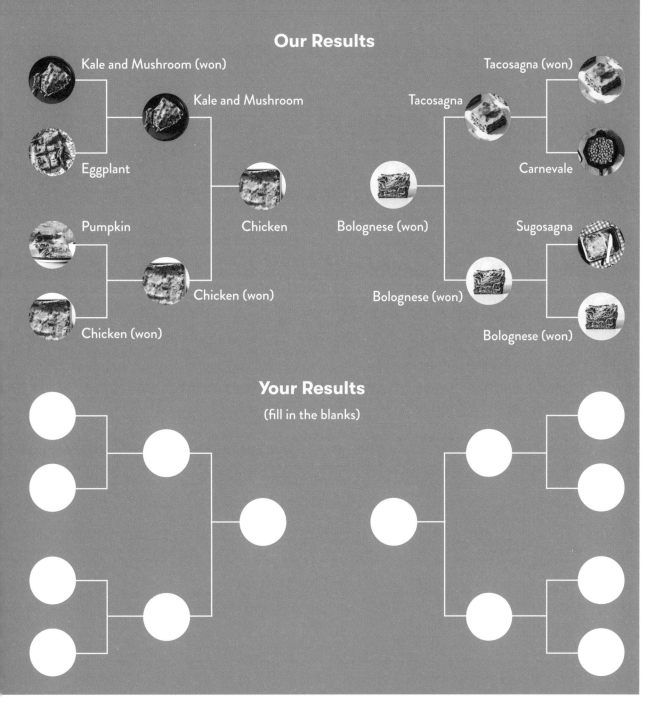

Kale and Mushroom (won)

Kale and Mushroom

Eggplant

Pumpkin

Chicken

Chicken (won)

Chicken (won)

Tacosagna (won)

Tacosagna

Carnevale

Bolognese (won)

Sugosagna

Bolognese (won)

Bolognese (won)

Your Results
(fill in the blanks)

Winner winner lasagna dinner! This is the lasagna that consistently won our bracket competition (see page 176), time after time. We did ordinary taste tests, single-blind taste tests, and double-blind taste tests and the results were always the same: This is our ultimate lasagna. With layers of tender noodles, silky rich extra umami–filled Bolognese sauce (thanks to our special secret ingredient, fish sauce), creamy besciamella, and a generous amount of Parmigiano, this is baked noodle perfection. Like all good things, this is a recipe that takes time. We like to break it into steps to make it more manageable: making the sauce the night before, then tackling the besciamella and assembly the next day.

So EXTRA IT CAN'T EVEN

THE ULTIMATE LASAGNA ALLA BOLOGNESE

Serves 8

1 tablespoon neutral oil

1 pound 50/50 ground beef and pork mix

4 ounces guanciale, finely chopped

Salt and freshly ground black pepper

1 large onion, peeled and finely chopped

1 carrot, finely chopped

2 ribs celery, finely chopped

¼ cup tomato paste

1 cup dry white wine

2 cups sodium-free beef stock

1 bay leaf

½ cup heavy (whipping) cream

½ tablespoon fish sauce, or to taste

1 batch Besciamella Sauce (page 175), warmed

1 pound dried or 2 pounds fresh lasagna noodles (see Note)

1 cup finely grated Parmigiano-Reggiano cheese

1. Heat the oil in a large Dutch oven or stockpot over medium-high heat. When it is hot, add the ground meat and guanciale and cook, stirring with a wooden spoon to break up the meat, until browned, 10 to 15 minutes. Taste and season with salt and pepper. Use a slotted spoon to transfer the meat to a bowl, reserving the rendered fat in the pan.

2. Return the pan to medium heat and add the onion, carrot, and celery. Cook, stirring occasionally, until the vegetables are soft and the onion translucent but not brown, 4 to 5 minutes. Stir in the tomato paste and cook until slightly caramelized, about 1 minute. Add the wine, stirring and scraping the bottom of the pan to release any browned bits, then let simmer, uncovered, until reduced by half, 6 to 8 minutes. Add the reserved meat along with the beef stock and bay leaf. Bring to a boil, then reduce the heat to low and simmer, partially covered and stirring occasionally, until thick and silky, at least 2 hours.

3. When the sauce is almost done, stir in the cream and fish sauce. Taste and season aggressively with salt and pepper—the sauce needs a little extra seasoning to stand up to the noodles. Discard the bay leaf.

4. Preheat your oven to 375°F.

5. Spread 1 cup of Bolognese sauce evenly on the bottom of a 9 x 13-inch baking dish (or any other similarly sized vessel; see page 174). Then build the first layer: Start with a single layer of noodles, followed by 1 cup of sauce and 1 cup of besciamella. Spread your sauces evenly to the edges, then dust evenly with ¼ cup of grated cheese. Repeat until you have built at least four layers (adapt these measures based on the size of your pan, making sure to end with the cheese).

6. Cover the lasagna with aluminum foil and bake for 30 minutes, then remove the foil and bake until the cheese is browned and the sauce is bubbling, 15 minutes more. Let it rest for at least 10 minutes before digging in.

Note: If you are using dried noodles, prepare them as directed on page 174. If you are using fresh lasagna noodles, you don't need to cook them. Simply layer them as directed.

tip!

If you own a pressure cooker, you can use it to make the Bolognese sauce: After adding the beef stock and bay leaf, cook on high pressure for 30 minutes.

Like the Sicilian rigatoni alla norma that inspired it, this meatless lasagna is light but full of flavor. It might seem odd that the eggplants are peeled and the tomatoes aren't, but the tomato skins add just the right amount of texture. Peeling eggplants is simple—use a vegetable peeler, and they'll peel just like a carrot. Choose Japanese eggplants as opposed to globe eggplants; the Japanese eggplants are sweet and mild and have far fewer seeds.

EGGPLANT YOUR FACE IN THIS

EGGPLANT LASAGNA ALLA NORMA

Serves 8

Note: If you are using dried noodles, prepare them as directed on page 174. If you are using fresh lasagna noodles, you don't need to cook them. Simply layer them as directed.

2 tablespoons olive oil

1 large onion, peeled and finely chopped

4 cloves garlic, peeled and pressed or minced

2 large Japanese eggplants (about 1½ pounds), peeled and sliced crosswise into 1-inch-thick slices

2 pints cherry tomatoes

Salt and freshly ground black pepper

2 cups sodium-free vegetable or chicken stock

2 tablespoons finely chopped fresh flat-leaf parsley

1 pound dried or 2 pounds fresh lasagna noodles (see Note)

1 batch Besciamella Sauce (page 175), warmed

½ cup finely grated Parmigiano-Reggiano cheese

1. Heat the oil in a large sauté pan or skillet over medium-high heat. Add the onion and garlic and cook, stirring occasionally, until soft and translucent, about 2 minutes. Add the eggplant and sear, stirring occasionally, until slightly caramelized, 4 to 5 minutes. Stir in the cherry tomatoes and season generously with salt and pepper. Add the stock and stir, scraping the bottom of the pan with a wooden spoon to release any browned bits. Reduce the heat to low and simmer until the tomatoes have burst and the eggplant is very tender, 15 to 20 minutes.

2. Break up the tomatoes and eggplant with the back of a spoon or potato masher. Turn the heat up to medium-high and cook until the mixture has reduced slightly, 5 to 6 minutes. Stir in the parsley and season to taste with salt and pepper.

3. Preheat your oven to 375°F.

4. Spread 1 cup of the eggplant sauce evenly on the bottom of a 9 x 13-inch baking dish (or any other similarly sized vessel; see page 174). Then build the first layer: Start with a bed of noodles, followed by 1 cup of sauce and 1 cup of besciamella. Spread the sauce evenly to the edges. Repeat until you have built at least four layers (adapt these measures based on the size of your pan). Top the noodles evenly with the Parmigiano.

5. Cover the lasagna with aluminum foil and bake for 30 minutes, then remove the foil and bake until the cheese is browned, another 15 minutes. Let it rest for at least 10 minutes before digging in.

This is fall cooking at its best: hearty and warming, with seasonal squash making an appearance. Silky pureed kabocha pumpkin flecked with sage is layered with ricotta and noodles in this meat-free lasagna. Of all the squashes, kabocha pumpkin is our squash of choice—it's slightly sweet and cooks up drier and fluffier than most other squashes; it's also small enough that a single pumpkin can be used up in one go.

PUMPKIN SAGE LASAGNA

2 tablespoons olive oil

2-pound kabocha, peeled, seeded, and cut into ½-inch pieces (about 3 cups)

1 onion, peeled and chopped

2 cloves garlic, peeled and pressed or minced

1 tablespoon finely chopped fresh sage

Salt and freshly ground black pepper

2 cups sodium-free vegetable or chicken stock

1 pound ricotta cheese

1 cup freshly grated Parmigiano-Reggiano cheese

1 large egg, lightly beaten

Pinch of freshly grated nutmeg

Finely grated zest of 1 lemon

1 pound dried or 2 pounds fresh lasagna noodles (see Note)

1 pound fresh mozzarella cheese, sliced into ¼-inch pieces

1. Heat the oil in a large sauté pan over medium-high heat. Add the kabocha, onion, garlic, and sage and cook, stirring occasionally, until the kabocha starts to brown at the edges, 8 to 10 minutes. Season with salt and pepper and then add the stock. Simmer until the pumpkin is soft and tender, 15 to 20 minutes. Let cool slightly, then puree with an immersion blender (or in a blender) until smooth. Adjust the seasoning if needed.

2. Meanwhile, stir together the ricotta with the Parmigiano, egg, nutmeg, and lemon zest in a small bowl. Season generously with salt and pepper.

3. Preheat your oven to 375°F.

4. Spread 1 cup of the kabocha sauce evenly on the bottom of a 9 x 13-inch baking dish (or any other similarly sized vessel; see page 174). Then build the first layer: Start with a bed of noodles, followed by 1 cup of sauce and one-quarter of the ricotta mixture, spreading both evenly to the edges. Repeat until you have built at least four layers (adapt these measures based on the size of your pan). Top the noodles evenly with the mozzarella.

5. Cover the lasagna with aluminum foil and bake for 30 minutes, then remove the foil and bake until the cheese is browned, 15 minutes more. Let it rest for at least 10 minutes before digging in.

Note: If you are using dried noodles, prepare them as directed on page 174. If you are using fresh lasagna noodles, you don't need to cook them. Simply layer them as directed.

Serves 8

5x Better

Top the lasagna with crispy sage leaves: While the lasagna bakes, fry sage leaves in a touch of oil in a medium pan over medium heat until they are crisp, 15 to 30 seconds per side. Let them drain on a paper towel, then top the lasagna with them after it comes out of the oven.

You can replace kabocha with any squash, such as butternut or acorn squash. While pumpkin and squash are fall harvest vegetables, most grocery stores stock them year round so you can feel those fall feels in the spring, summer, and winter!

Usually when people think of lasagna, they don't think of white lasagna. But they should—white lasagna is rich and savory and, for those who aren't a fan of tomatoes, it's kind of the best thing ever. This lasagna is like the tastiest chicken pot pie you'll ever eat, but even better because [dramatic pause] it has noodles and *two* kinds of cheese. If you go the distance and use fresh noodles, it becomes a simple one-pot lasagna with a rich and creamy chicken gravy. Not too bad, as lasagnas go.

COZY CHICKEN

CREAMY CHICKEN LASAGNA

5 tablespoons unsalted butter

1 medium onion, peeled and finely chopped

2 cloves garlic, peeled and pressed or minced

2 pounds boneless, skinless chicken thighs, cut into ½-inch pieces

½ cup all-purpose flour

2 cups sodium-free chicken stock

2 cups whole milk

¼ cup finely chopped fresh flat-leaf parsley

4 cups shredded low-moisture mozzarella cheese (about 1 pound)

Salt and freshly ground black pepper

1 pound dried or 2 pounds fresh lasagna noodles (see Note)

1 cup finely grated Parmigiano-Reggiano cheese

1. Preheat your oven to 375°F.

2. Melt 1 tablespoon of the butter in a large sauté pan over medium heat. Add the onion and garlic and cook until soft and translucent, 2 to 3 minutes. Add the chicken and lightly sear, then add the remaining 4 tablespoons of butter. When the butter has melted, sprinkle in the flour and stir until the flour coats the chicken evenly. Add the chicken stock in a thin stream, whisking constantly. Stir in the milk and let simmer until thickened, about 5 minutes. Remove the pan from the heat and add the parsley and 3 cups of the shredded mozzarella. Stir until the cheese is melted, then season generously with salt and pepper.

3. Spread 1 cup of the creamy chicken sauce evenly on the bottom of a 9 x 13-inch baking dish (or any other similarly sized vessel; see page 174). Then build the first layer: Start with a bed of noodles, followed by 1 cup of sauce, spreading it evenly to the edges, and ¼ cup of grated Parmigiano. Repeat until you have built at least four layers (adapt these measures based on the size of your pan). Top the noodles with the remaining 1 cup of mozzarella.

4. Cover the lasagna with aluminum foil and bake for 30 minutes, then remove the foil and bake until the cheese is browned, another 15 minutes. Let it rest for at least 10 minutes before digging in.

Note: If you are using dried noodles, prepare them as directed on page 174. If you are using fresh lasagna noodles, you don't need to cook them. Simply layer them as directed.

Serves 8

Kale and mushrooms go hand in hand in this creamy umami-rich vegetarian lasagna. The hardiness of kale stands up well to baking, and its slightly bitter notes are a nice foil for the rich, savory mushroom sauce. Be sure to brown the mushrooms in batches, letting them sear in place so they caramelize instead of steam.

KALE-ING ME SOFTLY

KALE AND MUSHROOM LASAGNA

Serves 8

8 tablespoons (1 stick) unsalted butter

1 medium onion, peeled and finely chopped

2 cloves garlic, peeled and pressed or minced

12 ounces kale, stemmed and finely chopped (about 2 bunches)

Salt and freshly ground black pepper

1½ pounds mushrooms, trimmed and sliced

½ cup all-purpose flour

4 cups (1 quart) whole milk

2 cups finely grated Parmigiano-Reggiano cheese

1 pound dried or 2 pounds fresh lasagna noodles (see Note)

tip!

The mushroom choice here makes the dish, so you can go any way you'd like. We don't specify the mushrooms because, if we're being honest, we often buy the little containers of mushroom medley at the grocery store that contain a mix of mushroom varieties.

1. Preheat your oven to 375°F.

2. Melt 1 tablespoon of the butter in a large sauté pan over medium heat. Add the onion and garlic and cook until soft and translucent, 2 to 3 minutes. Add the kale and cook until wilted, 2 to 3 minutes. Season with salt and pepper. Transfer to a bowl and set aside.

3. In the same pan, melt 2 tablespoons of the butter over medium heat. Add the mushrooms and cook without disturbing until golden brown on the bottom, 2 to 3 minutes. Flip and stir the mushrooms, then let cook until browned on the other side, 2 to 3 minutes. Add the remaining 5 tablespoons of butter and melt, then sprinkle on the flour and stir until the flour coats the mushrooms evenly. Add the milk in a thin stream, whisking constantly. Simmer until thickened, 5 minutes, then stir in 1½ cups of the Parmigiano. Remove the pan from the heat and season generously with salt and pepper.

4. Spread 1 cup of the mushroom sauce evenly on the bottom of a 9 x 13-inch baking dish (or any other similarly sized vessel; see page 174). Then build the first layer: Start with a bed of noodles, followed by ¼ cup of the kale mixture and 1 cup of mushroom sauce. Repeat until you have built at least four layers (adapt these measures based on the size of your pan). Sprinkle the remaining ½ cup of Parmigiano on top.

5. Cover the lasagna with aluminum foil and bake for 30 minutes, then remove the foil and bake until the cheese is browned, another 15 minutes. Let it rest for at least 10 minutes before digging in.

Note: If you are using dried noodles, prepare them as directed on page 174. If you are using fresh lasagna noodles, you don't need to cook them. Simply layer them as directed.

This lasagna is sort of a quicker, porkier version of the lasagna alla Bolognese on page 178. The base is an all-pork sauce with a hint of tomato. It has the benefit of a shorter simmer time and a special ingredient whisked into the besciamella: mascarpone. This Italian version of cream cheese has a slightly higher fat content that gives this sauce a creamy lusciousness.

SUGOSAGNA

LASAGNA WITH CREAMY TOMATO PORK SUGO

1 tablespoon olive oil

4 ounces guanciale, finely chopped

1 medium onion, peeled and finely chopped

2 cloves garlic, peeled and pressed or minced

1 carrot, finely chopped

1 pound ground pork

¼ cup tomato paste

1 cup dry white wine

1 bay leaf

2 cups (1 pint) whole milk, plus extra as needed

Salt and freshly ground black pepper

1 batch Besciamella Sauce (page 175)

1 pound mascarpone cheese

1 pound dried or 2 pounds fresh lasagna noodles (see Note)

1. Heat the oil in a large sauté pan over medium-high heat. Add the guanciale and fry until crispy, 4 to 5 minutes. Add the onion, garlic, and carrot and cook, stirring occasionally, until soft and very caramelized, 8 to 10 minutes. Add the ground pork and tomato paste and cook for 2 minutes, stirring occasionally. Add the wine, stirring and scraping the bottom of the pan to release any browned bits, then simmer until reduced by about half, 3 to 4 minutes. Finally, stir in the bay leaf and milk and simmer over low heat, partially covered, for 1 hour. Season generously with salt and pepper and discard the bay leaf.

2. Preheat your oven to 375°F.

3. Gently heat the besciamella in a medium saucepan over low heat, 4 to 5 minutes, loosening it with 1 to 2 tablespoons of milk if necessary. Stir in the mascarpone until smooth and creamy.

4. Spread 1 cup of the sugo evenly on the bottom of a 9 x 13-inch baking dish (or any other similarly sized vessel; see page 174). Then build the first layer: Start with a bed of noodles, followed by 1 cup of the sugo and 1 cup of the mascarpone besciamella. Spread the sauces evenly to the edges. Repeat until you have built at least four layers (adapt these measures based on the size of your pan).

5. Cover the lasagna with aluminum foil and bake for 30 minutes, then remove the foil and bake until the top is browned, another 15 minutes. Let it rest for at least 10 minutes before slicing.

Note: If you are using dried noodles, prepare them as directed on page 174. If you are using fresh lasagna noodles, you don't need to cook them. Simply layer them as directed.

Serves 8

5x Better

Use ground veal, duck, beef, or even a mix instead of the pork.

The inspiration for this lasagna was taco night. Not street tacos or authentic Mexican ones, nope—we're talking about the tacos of childhood: hard, fluorescent yellow shells filled with heavily spiced, way-to-salty ground meat and topped with iceberg lettuce, tomato, and shredded cheese. We swapped noodles for the taco shells here, but otherwise we kept pretty much everything else the same, minus the store-bought taco mix (we made our own version instead). The result: a flavor bomb that will take you right back to when you were young.

TACOSAGNA

A RIDICULOUS TACO LASAGNA THAT SOMEHOW WORKS

1 tablespoon neutral oil

1 medium onion, peeled and diced

2 pounds lean ground beef

2 tablespoons tomato paste

1 teaspoon all-purpose flour

1 teaspoon onion powder

1 teaspoon garlic powder

1 teaspoon ground cumin

1 teaspoon paprika

½ teaspoon dried oregano

½ teaspoon ground cayenne pepper

Salt and freshly ground black pepper

1 pound dried or 2 pounds fresh lasagna noodles (see Note)

4 cups shredded Mexican four-cheese mix

1. Heat the oil in a large sauté pan over medium-high heat. Add the onion and cook, stirring occasionally, until translucent, 2 to 3 minutes. Add the beef and cook, stirring occasionally, until browned, 7 to 10 minutes. Add the tomato paste, flour, onion powder, garlic powder, cumin, paprika, oregano, and cayenne and stir to combine. Add 1½ cups of water and let simmer until everything comes together in a loose sauce, 3 to 4 minutes. Season with salt and black pepper.

2. Preheat your oven to 375°F.

3. Spread 1 cup of the taco meat sauce evenly on the bottom of a 9 x 13-inch baking dish (or any other similarly sized vessel; see page 174). Then build the first layer: Start with a bed of noodles, followed by 1 cup of sauce, spreading it evenly to the edges, then 1 cup of shredded cheese. Repeat until you have built at least four layers, making sure cheese is on top (adapt these measures based on the size of your pan).

4. Cover the lasagna with aluminum foil and bake for 30 minutes, then remove the foil and bake until the cheese is browned, another 15 minutes. Let it rest for at least 10 minutes before digging in.

Note: If you are using dried noodles, prepare them as directed on page 174. If you are using fresh lasagna noodles, you don't need to cook them. Simply layer them as directed.

Serves 8

Toppings

Shredded lettuce
Chopped tomatoes
Sour cream

tip!

If you don't have all the spices on hand, taco seasoning is a perfectly acceptable alternative. Be sure to adjust your salt to match—taco seasoning is often aggressively salty already.

This over-the-top lasagna is incredibly fun: a slow-cooked tomato–pork rib sauce, tiny meatballs, pockets of melty mozzarella, fresh ricotta, and layers and layers of noodles. Lasagna was born in Naples, so it's only right that their regional version is spectacular. Traditionally made for Carnevale (i.e., Carnival, Italy's version of Mardi Gras), Lasagna di Carnevale is meant to be a break-the-bank kind of meal—the kind you dream about when you're not supposed to be eating. This lasagna can be a bit of a project, but you can divide it up over two days: Make the meatballs and sauce a day ahead and keep them in the fridge until you assemble the lasagna the next day.

LASAGNA DI CARNEVALE

AN EVEN MORE RIDICULOUS LASAGNA WITH MEATBALLS INSIDE

Serves 8

2 pounds baby back pork ribs, trimmed into sections

Salt and freshly ground black pepper

2 tablespoons olive oil, plus extra for oiling the baking sheet

1 medium onion, peeled and chopped

4 cloves garlic, peeled and pressed or minced

¼ cup tomato paste

½ cup dry white wine

1 can (28 ounces) crushed tomatoes

3 sprigs fresh basil

½ cup panko or plain dried breadcrumbs

1 pound ground pork

2 large eggs

6 cups finely grated Parmigiano-Reggiano cheese

1 pound dried or 2 pounds fresh lasagna noodles (see Note)

1 pound ricotta cheese

1 pound fresh mozzarella cheese, cut into ½-inch cubes

¼ cup finely chopped fresh flat-leaf parsley

1. Season the ribs all over with salt and pepper. Heat the oil in a large pot over medium-high heat, add the ribs, and cook, flipping once, until the ribs are deeply brown, 4 to 5 minutes per side. Add the onion, 2 cloves of the garlic, and the tomato paste and cook, stirring occasionally, until the onion and garlic are tender, 2 to 3 minutes. Add the wine and simmer, stirring and scraping the bottom of the pan to release any browned bits. When the wine is reduced by half, 3 to 4 minutes, add the crushed tomatoes, basil sprigs, and enough water to cover the ribs. Simmer on low, partially covered, until the rib meat starts to fall off the bone, about 2 hours.

2. Transfer the ribs to a cutting board and pull the meat off the bones. Roughly chop the meat, then stir it back into the sauce, discarding the bones and basil. Adjust the seasoning if needed.

3. Preheat your oven to 375°F. Line a rimmed baking sheet with aluminum foil and coat it lightly with oil.

4. Combine the panko, ground pork, eggs, the remaining garlic, 2 cups of the Parmigiano, and ¼ teaspoon each of salt and pepper in a large bowl and mix gently with your hands into a homogenous mixture. Roll the meat mixture into very tiny meatballs, each about the size of a hazelnut, and place in a single layer on the prepared baking sheet. Bake the meatballs, flipping once, until cooked through, about 20 minutes.

Continued on page 194 ⟶

5. Spread 1 cup of the tomato–pork rib sauce evenly on the bottom of a 9 x 13-inch baking dish (or any other similarly sized vessel; see page 174). Then build the first layer: Start with a bed of noodles, followed by 1 cup of sauce, spreading it to the edges. Evenly scatter one-third of the meatballs, one-third of the ricotta, and one-quarter of the mozzarella cubes, like you're making a pizza. Lightly dust with 1 cup of Parmigiano and 1 tablespoon of parsley. Repeat until you have built at least three layers (adapt these measures based on the size of your pan). Finish with a final layer of noodles and the remaining sauce, mozzarella cubes, Parmigiano, and parsley.

6. Cover the lasagna with aluminum foil and bake for 30 minutes, then remove the foil and bake until the cheese is browned on top, another 15 minutes. Let it rest for at least 10 minutes before digging in.

Note: If you are using dried noodles, prepare them as directed on page 174. If you are using fresh lasagna noodles, you don't need to cook them. Simply layer them as directed.

7

LIVING YOUR BEST NOODLE LIFE

Sometimes you just can't get noodles off your mind.

You think about them constantly. You eat them at least once a day. You're all about that noodle life. These are the noodles you dream about: soupy strands lifted in a noodle pull, bowls of spoonable satisfaction, plates of perfection. If noodles were a destination, this chapter would be on your must-visit list. These are our ultimate recipes, the ones we save for special occasions and rainy days. Some of them are time-consuming, some have esoteric ingredients, and some are a bit challenging to get right, but what they all share is an undeniable deliciousness that more than makes up for the work involved. We're ending on a high note so you can go forth and live your best noodle life.

Classic Bolognese is made with a mix of ground meats, but use whole cuts, seared to build flavor, then slow braised to break them down and richly infuse the sauce. The true Bolognese secret ingredient, chicken livers, gives this sauce that extra hint of umami, while soy and fish sauce give it another layer of intensity.

THE ULTIMATE MEAT SAUCE

OVER-THE-TOP BOLOGNESE WITH PAPPARDELLE

1 pound boneless beef chuck steak

1 pound boneless pork shoulder

1 pound boneless lamb shoulder

Salt and freshly ground black pepper

2 tablespoons olive oil

4 ounces guanciale, cubed

1 medium onion, peeled and finely chopped

1 carrot, finely chopped

2 ribs celery, finely chopped

4 cloves garlic, peeled and pressed or minced

¼ pound chicken livers, finely chopped

3 tablespoons chopped fresh flat-leaf parsley

1 teaspoon fennel seeds, crushed

¼ cup tomato paste

1 cup dry white wine

1 can (28 ounces) crushed tomatoes

2½ cups sodium-free beef stock

2 bay leaves

½ cup heavy cream

1 cup grated Parmigiano-Reggiano cheese

1 tablespoon fish sauce

1 tablespoon light soy sauce

24 ounces fresh pappardelle

1. Preheat your oven to 300°F.

2. Season the beef, pork, and lamb generously on all sides with salt and pepper. Heat the oil in a large Dutch oven over medium-high heat and sear the meats (in batches if needed to avoid crowding the pot) until deeply brown on all sides, 8 to 10 minutes per batch. Remove to a plate and set aside.

3. Reduce the heat to medium and add the guanciale to the pot. Cook until crispy, 4 to 5 minutes, then add the onion, carrot, celery, garlic, livers, parsley, and fennel seeds. Cook until the onion is soft and translucent, 1 to 2 minutes, then stir in the tomato paste and cook until slightly caramelized, 2 to 3 minutes. Add the wine, stirring and scraping the bottom of the pan to release any browned bits, and turn the heat up to high. Simmer until the wine is reduced by half, 6 to 8 minutes. Add the crushed tomatoes, beef stock, bay leaves, and the browned meats. When the mixture returns to a simmer, transfer the pot, uncovered, to the oven and braise until the meats are very fork-tender, about 2 hours.

4. Remove the pot from the oven. Find and discard the bay leaves. Transfer the meat to a large bowl, let cool slightly, then shred or roughly chop it. Stir the meat back into the sauce along with the cream, Parmigiano, fish sauce, and soy sauce. Adjust the seasoning to taste.

5. Bring a large pot of salted water to a boil over high heat. Add the pappardelle and cook until it just starts to float, 2 to 3 minutes.

Continued on next page ——→

Serves 4 (with enough sauce for 8 to 10 servings)

Toppings

Finely grated Parmigiano
Freshly cracked black pepper
Crushed red pepper flakes

Make It Ahead

Make the sauce ahead of time (you can even double it) and sauce your noodles as needed—the sauce will keep in the fridge, tightly covered, for up to 5 days and for up to 1 month in the freezer (divide it into ½-cup portions for easily defrosted individual servings). Gently reheat in a saucepan over medium-low heat, loosening with a touch of cream, if needed.

A splatter shield—which looks like the love child of a fine-mesh sieve and a tennis racket—can help keep things neat during the meat-browning step.

6. Meanwhile, transfer 2 cups of the sauce to a large skillet and bring to a simmer over medium heat, then reduce the heat to medium-low. (Store the remaining sauce—see Make It Ahead.) When the pappardelle is done, drain it well, reserving 1 cup of the pasta cooking water, and transfer the pappardelle to the skillet with the sauce. Cook until the pappardelle is coated and the sauce is glossy, about 1 minute, adding the reserved pasta water a tablespoon at a time if it looks dry. Serve immediately.

Duck is surprisingly easy to cook. In terms of meats, it's the highest reward for the lowest effort. Hank Shaw—the author of *Hunt, Gather, Cook*—has the easiest roast duck leg method in the game. He starts off by poking some holes in the duck skin with a sharp paring knife (this gives the fat somewhere to go when it liquifies during roasting), and then he puts the leg in a very small baking dish before sticking it in the oven. The duck fat slowly renders out and surrounds the duck, cooking it in a bath of its own fat instead of dry oven heat. It's an easy duck confit without having to go out and buy duck fat.

REALLY EASY DUCK CONFIT

ZITI WITH DUCK, SAGE, AND DUCK FAT BROWN BUTTER SAUCE

1 duck leg (9 to 10 ounces)

Salt

6 ounces dried ziti

3 tablespoons unsalted butter

10 fresh sage leaves

2 tablespoons finely grated Parmigiano-Reggiano cheese

1. Pat the duck leg dry with paper towels, then lightly score or pierce the skin with a sharp paring knife. Salt it generously, and put it in a small baking dish or oven-proof saucepan that fits the leg as snugly as possible. Place the baking dish in a cold oven and turn the heat to 300°F. When the oven reaches temp, set a timer and roast for 2 hours. At this point, the duck should be lightly golden brown and fork-tender. If the duck meat doesn't shred easily, continue roasting it for another 15 minutes.

2. Bring a large pot of salted water to a boil over high heat. Add the ziti and cook according to the package directions until it is 3 minutes shy of al dente. Drain well, reserving 1 cup of the pasta cooking water.

3. Meanwhile, remove the duck leg from the oven and transfer it to a cutting board. When it has cooled to the touch, debone it. Reserve the bone for stock or discard it; reserve the rendered fat in a small glass measuring cup for Step 5. Separate the skin and meat and roughly chop both. Set aside the meat.

4. Transfer the chopped duck skin to a large dry skillet over medium-low heat and crisp up the skin, stirring occasionally to ensure even browning. Once the skin is deeply brown, 4 to 5 minutes, remove it from the skillet and set it aside. Add any rendered fat to your measuring cup from the previous step.

Serves 2

Toppings

Finely grated Parmigiano
Freshly ground black pepper
Flaky sea salt

Continued on page 205 ⟶

5. Return the skillet to medium-low heat and add the butter and 2 tablespoons of the reserved duck fat. When the mixture starts to foam, add the sage leaves and fry, turning once, until crispy, 15 to 30 seconds depending on their size. Transfer the leaves as they cook to a paper towel to drain (keep the butter mixture on the heat).

6. By now the butter mixture should be lightly brown and nutty. Add the pasta, ¼ cup of pasta water, and duck meat and turn the heat up to medium-high. Cook, tossing gently and adding pasta water a tablespoon at a time as needed, until a glossy sauce has formed and the pasta is al dente, about 3 minutes. Remove from the heat and stir in the Parmigiano and half of the duck skin.

7. Top with the remaining duck skin and the fried sage, and serve immediately.

This is a sweet, spicy, and complex pasta that's so dangerously delicious we only make a portion or two at a time. The key flavor comes from the caramelized pork belly. Caramelizing sugar is an essential technique in Vietnamese cooking. Unlike the creamy caramels found in French cuisine, Vietnamese caramel contains only sugar with water or oil and adds a unique complexity and sweetness to a variety of dishes. While the traditional method for making Vietnamese caramel is mastered over years of practice, this version is easy and foolproof and can't go too burnt or bitter.

PORK. THE ONE YOU LOVE.

CRACKED BLACK PEPPER AND PORK BELLY FUSILLI BUCATI

1 tablespoon neutral oil

1 shallot, peeled and finely minced

4 cloves garlic, peeled and pressed or minced

2 tablespoons sugar

1 pound pork belly, cut into ½-inch matchsticks

2 tablespoons fish sauce

Freshly cracked black pepper

Salt

12 ounces dried fusilli bucati

1. Preheat your oven to 300°F.

2. Heat the oil in an oven-proof pot with a lid over medium heat. Once it is shimmering, add the shallot, garlic, sugar, and pork and fry, stirring only once to ensure everything is coated, until the mixture starts to bubble, about 2 minutes. Remove the pan from the heat and stir in the fish sauce, 1 cup of water, and as much black pepper as you can handle, but at least 1 teaspoon. Cover and transfer to the oven. Braise until the pork is tender, about 1 hour.

3. Bring a large pot of salted water to a boil over high heat. Add the fusilli bucati and cook according to the package directions until it is al dente. Drain well.

4. Remove the pot from the oven and place it on the stove over high heat. Bring the pork mixture up to a boil and cook to caramelize the pork, about 2 minutes. Gently toss the pasta into the sauce until well coated. Serve immediately.

Serves 4

Toppings

Sliced green onions
Crispy fried onions (see page 239)
Fresh Herbs (see page 122)

Vietnamese caramelized meats are traditionally served very sweet and very spicy. Although we've left out the typical crushed Thai chilies, if you're feeling daring, toss one or two with the finished sauce to balance out the sweetness of the dish.

Food Wars is an over-the-top Japanese culinary school–themed manga series that was turned into a TV show. The main character, Soma, invents an amazing curry meatball mapo tofu ramen to win a competition. We thought Soma's idea sounded so good, we decided we had to try it in real life. This is the result, inspired by Soma's dish but with a couple of changes: We swapped the ramen for pasta and ditched the curry meatballs (they seemed extraneous), but strands of homemade pasta tossed in a spicy mapo sauce? Move over, mapo tofu rice, because mapo tofu pasta is here to stay.

THE SPICE MUST FLOW

SPICY SICHUAN MAPO TOFU CHITARRA

Serves 2

Toppings

Sliced green onions
Crispy fried shallots
 (see page 239)

5x Better

Topping this with some freshly cracked toasted Sichuan peppercorns will give it that authentic mouth-numbing Sichuan spiciness.

Salt

2 portions (12 ounces) Spaghetti alla Chitarra (page 13) or fresh long pasta of your choice

1 tablespoon neutral oil

¼ pound ground pork

1 tablespoon doubanjiang (see page 237), chopped

2 cloves garlic, peeled and pressed or minced

1 cup sodium-free chicken stock

1 tablespoon soy sauce

1 tablespoon cornstarch, whisked into 2 tablespoons water

1 package (14 to 16 ounces) soft tofu, cut into ½-inch cubes

1. Bring a medium pot of salted water to a boil over high heat. Add the spaghetti and cook until it just starts to float, 2 to 3 minutes. Drain well.

2. Heat the oil in a medium wok (or large nonstick skillet) over medium-high heat. When the oil is hot and shimmery, add the pork and cook, breaking it up with a wooden spoon, until lightly browned, 2 to 3 minutes.

3. Reduce the heat to medium and stir in the doubanjiang. Add the garlic and cook, stirring until fragrant, about 1 minute. Add the stock and soy sauce and turn the heat up to high so everything comes up to a simmer. Stir in the cornstarch slurry and simmer until the sauce is thick and glossy, about 1 minute, then remove from the heat.

4. Add the noodles and toss until coated. Gently stir in the tofu. Serve immediately.

HELLO
my name is

RAMEN

Ramen needs no introduction. It's been a force of nature in the American restaurant scene since the first Momofuku Noodle Bar opened up in NYC around 2004. Nowadays, even our Japanese ramen nerd friends agree that you can find pretty great ramen everywhere from Providence, Rhode Island, to San Francisco, and many, many cities in between. In America, the general thinking goes that there are four major categories of ramen: salt, soy, miso, and tonkotsu. But in Tokyo, the spiritual home of ramen, there are thousands. We've had bowls ranging from Hainanese chicken interpreted as ramen to lamb ramen to sesame ramen. Ramen is one of the few homegrown Japanese dishes that invites innovation. Cooks are encouraged and rewarded for experimenting within its framework of tare, broth, noodles, and chashu (see page 212).

Ramen is a complex beast with a lot of moving parts. This is everything that goes into our ramen.

1 Broth and Tare

The trick to really great ramen is in the body of its broth. Ramen broth is thick; it's very rare to find a thin ramen, and even the most delicately seasoned, clarified ramen will still have a wonderfully smooth and rich texture that's perfect for imbuing the noodles with flavor in a way most other soups cannot.

Tare is concentrated flavoring, and ramen's secret weapon. When you keep ramen broth at a rolling boil, as you must to give it its signature body, you deplete the liquid of a lot of taste and complexity. The flavor literally dissipates into the air. Splitting the soup into its components—broth and concentrated flavoring (tare)—allows you to simmer the broth for hours, then add the flavors at the very last minute when building the bowl.

2 Noodles

Ramen noodles are made specific to the regional origin and style of the ramen. They can range in thickness and texture from super-thin, ultra-firm Hakata-style noodles to thick, chewy udon-size tsukemen noodles, and everything in between.

3 Egg

The iconic ramen egg first hit America in a big way about 15 years ago, but to this day it remains a mystery to many. This symbol of technical expertise is actually super simple—it's just a 7-minute egg that's refrigerated and marinated— yet super impressive when done right.

4 Chashu

While chashu is traditionally made with roast pork (chashu is a Japanese interpretation of the classic Chinese char siu roast pork; see page 131), nowadays chashu refers to any meat component of ramen, from sous-vide fish to fried chicken to, more often these days, a mix of multiple meats.

5 Menma

Some people instinctively dislike the pickled bamboo that comes with ramen, and that's probably because they've never had it properly prepared. It should be freshly pickled and offer a subtle acidity to offset the richness of the other ingredients.

6 Wood Ear Mushrooms

You don't always get these in a bowl of ramen, but they're always welcome. Wood ear mushrooms are an easy component to prepare, and though they don't taste like very much, they excel in the texture department, adding a bright, fresh crunch.

7 Nori

Nori is underrated in ramen and more than just a garnish. A good sheet of nori provides sweetness and a hint of the sea that benefit all kinds of ramen.

RAMEN

This is our basic Japanese marinade. It's a beautifully unfinicky and versatile marinade that you can use for everything from soaking the ramen eggs and marinating the menma to braising the chashu. The key to this recipe is to use the best-quality bonito flakes you can find—ideally from Japan, with large flakes roughly an inch wide. You can scale this recipe as much or as little as you need. If you make this in advance, you can strain it for easier use (it will keep in an airtight jar in the refrigerator for up to a week), but in a pinch, you can make this recipe right when you need to marinate something and just sort of brush off the bonito flakes when you're done.

Basic Japanese Marinade

½ cup Japanese soy
sauce (see page 235)

½ cup mirin

½ cup cooking sake

½ cup best-quality
bonito flakes

**Makes 1½ cups, or
enough to make
1 batch each of
pickles, chashu,
and eggs**

Combine all of the ingredients in a small saucepan and warm over low heat until it is just below a boil, 3 to 4 minutes. (Alternatively, microwave the liquids for 1 to 2 minutes in a small microwave-safe bowl, then add the bonito flakes.) Let stand for at least 10 minutes; 2 to 3 hours is better. Strain before use if possible.

Marinated pickles play an important part in the ramen universe, adding crunch and acid to offset the richness of the broth. The technique that follows is the same no matter what vegetable you pick. We favor canned baby corn, canned bamboo shoots, and dried wood ear mushrooms, but you can use any pickled vegetables you'd like (see the Note on making your own).

Marinated Vegetables

8 ounces canned vegetables such as bamboo shoots or baby corn, drained

½ cup Basic Japanese Marinade (page 214)

Makes 8 ounces

1. Place the vegetables and marinade in a small saucepan and add enough water to cover. Bring to a boil over high heat and then immediately remove from the heat.

2. Transfer to an airtight container, add extra water as needed to cover, and refrigerate. The pickles will keep for up to 1 week.

Note: If you want to quick-pickle your own vegetables, you can make a brine by combining 1 cup rice vinegar with 1 tablespoon sugar and 1 teaspoon salt in a small saucepan. Bring the mixture to a boil, pour into a small pint jar, and add your vegetables. Top up with water and wait a couple of hours (2 days is ideal), then remove the pickles from the jar and marinate as directed above.

In Japan, the days of getting ramen topped with dry pieces of pork belly are long gone. Instead you'll get carefully selected cuts of ultra-high-quality meats that have been cooked sous-vide to perfection. The secret to getting a really good-looking piece of chashu is to wrap the meat tightly after cooking and refrigerate it for at least an hour, and preferably overnight. This allows the meat to rest and firm up again—it's the difference between a great chashu and pulled pork (or chicken or beef, for that matter).

Basic Chashu

1 pound of your favorite boneless cut of meat (we prefer a well-marbled, trimmed pork shoulder, a small beef chuck roast, or trimmed chicken breasts)

½ cup Basic Japanese Marinade (page 214)

1. Preheat your oven to 200°F.

2. Place the meat in a snug-fitting, ovenproof pot and add the marinade and enough water to cover the meat by 1 inch. Bring to a boil over high heat. Once it is boiling, loosely cover and transfer the pot to the oven and cook until an instant-read thermometer in the center of the meat reads 150°F, 1 to 2 hours, depending on the starting temperature of your meat.

3. Remove the meat from the pot and let it cool completely, then wrap it tightly in plastic wrap and refrigerate it for at least 1 hour (overnight is better) before slicing.

Makes 1 pound (enough for 4 bowls)

After slicing the chashu, warm it in the simmering ramen broth to get it up to temperature before building your bowl.

A ramen egg is an easy thing to make and always impressive. As long as you've mastered peeling a soft egg, you've got it down.

Ramen Eggs

4 large eggs

½ cup Basic Japanese Marinade (page 214)

1. Bring a large pot of water to a boil over high heat. Using a slotted spoon, carefully lower each egg into the water. Set a timer for 7 minutes and 45 seconds.

2. While the eggs are cooking, prepare an ice water bath in a large bowl. Separately, fill a tall glass jar with the marinade.

3. When the eggs are done, transfer them to the ice bath. When they have cooled, crack each one at the base and carefully peel, then place the peeled egg in the marinade.

4. When all the eggs have been placed in the marinade, top off the marinade with water, cover, and refrigerate for at least 24 hours before using. Ramen eggs are traditionally served cold as a counterpoint to the piping-hot soup and noodles.

Makes 4

If you like to serve the eggs sliced in half, you can get cleaner cuts by using a sharp paring knife and washing the knife after every cut. Alternatively, use unflavored dental floss. We prefer to slice the eggs along the equator to make slicing even easier. This makes for a more unique presentation as well.

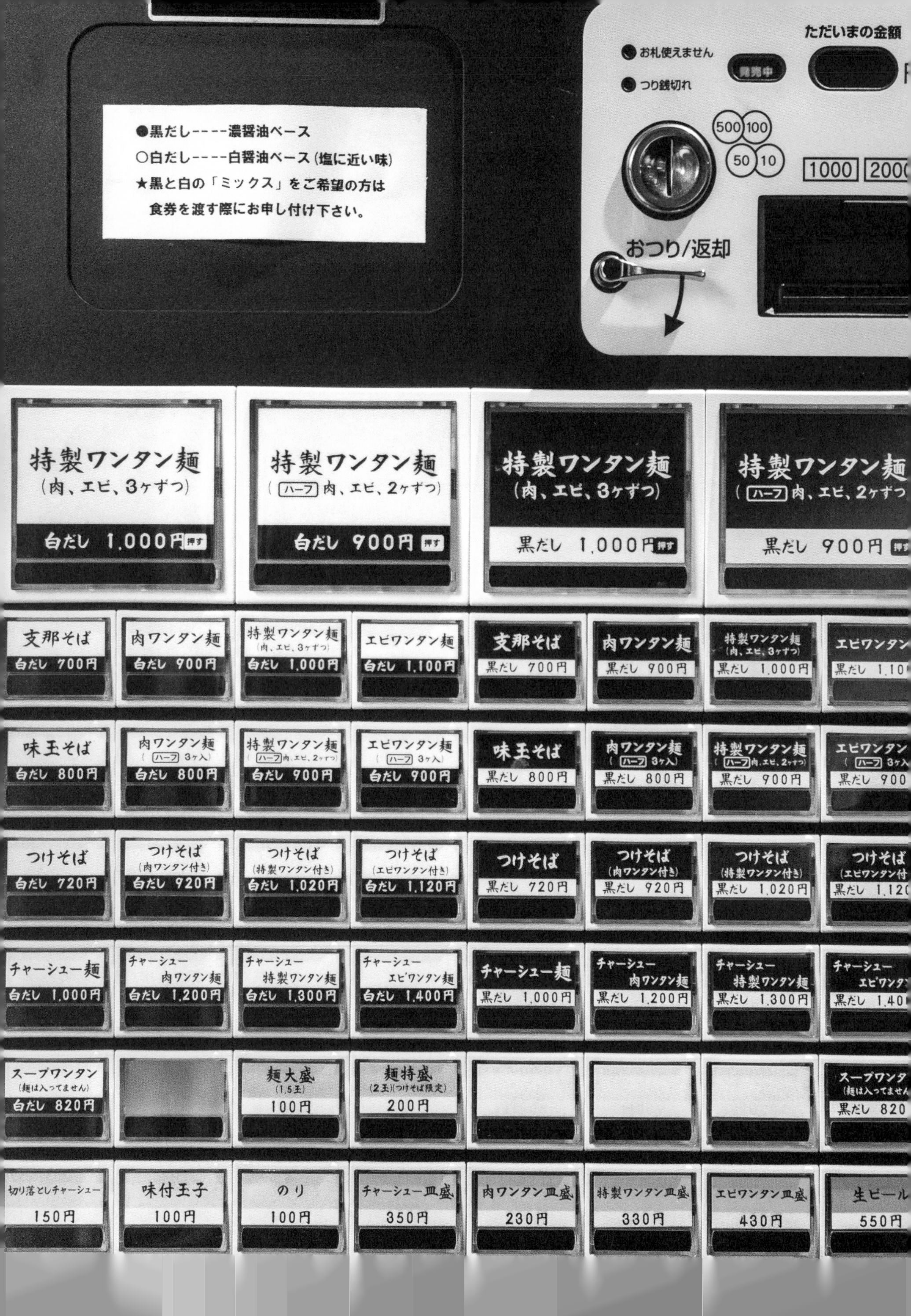

● お札使えません
● つり銭切れ

発売中

ただいまの金額

500 100
50 10
1000 2000

おつり/返却

特製ワンタン麺 (肉、エビ、3ヶずつ) 白だし 1,000円 押す	特製ワンタン麺 (ハーフ 肉、エビ、2ヶずつ) 白だし 900円 押す	特製ワンタン麺 (肉、エビ、3ヶずつ) 黒だし 1,000円 押す	特製ワンタン麺 (ハーフ 肉、エビ、2ヶずつ) 黒だし 900円 押す

支那そば 白だし 700円	肉ワンタン麺 白だし 900円	特製ワンタン麺 (肉、エビ、3ヶずつ) 白だし 1,000円	エビワンタン麺 白だし 1,100円	支那そば 黒だし 700円	肉ワンタン麺 黒だし 900円	特製ワンタン麺 (肉、エビ、3ヶずつ) 黒だし 1,000円	エビワンタン 黒だし 1,10
味玉そば 白だし 800円	肉ワンタン麺 (ハーフ 3ヶ入) 白だし 800円	特製ワンタン麺 (ハーフ 肉、エビ、2ヶずつ) 白だし 900円	エビワンタン麺 (ハーフ 3ヶ入) 白だし 900円	味玉そば 黒だし 800円	肉ワンタン麺 (ハーフ 3ヶ入) 黒だし 800円	特製ワンタン麺 (ハーフ 肉、エビ、2ヶずつ) 黒だし 900円	エビワンタン (ハーフ 3ヶ入) 黒だし 900円
つけそば 白だし 720円	つけそば (肉ワンタン付き) 白だし 920円	つけそば (特製ワンタン付き) 白だし 1,020円	つけそば (エビワンタン付き) 白だし 1,120円	つけそば 黒だし 720円	つけそば (肉ワンタン付き) 黒だし 920円	つけそば (特製ワンタン付き) 黒だし 1,020円	つけそば (エビワンタン付 黒だし 1,120
チャーシュー麺 白だし 1,000円	チャーシュー 肉ワンタン麺 白だし 1,200円	チャーシュー 特製ワンタン麺 白だし 1,300円	チャーシュー エビワンタン麺 白だし 1,400円	チャーシュー麺 黒だし 1,000円	チャーシュー 肉ワンタン麺 黒だし 1,200円	チャーシュー 特製ワンタン麺 黒だし 1,300円	チャーシュー エビワンタン 黒だし 1,40
スープワンタン (麺は入ってません) 白だし 820円		麺大盛 (1.5玉) 100円	麺特盛 (2玉)(つけそば限定) 200円				スープワンタ (麺は入ってません) 黒だし 820
切り落としチャーシュー 150円	味付玉子 100円	のり 100円	チャーシュー皿盛 350円	肉ワンタン皿盛 230円	特製ワンタン皿盛 330円	エビワンタン皿盛 430円	生ビール 550円

How to Order Ramen in Japan

There are noodles everywhere in Japan, but perhaps the most ubiquitous—seemingly on every street corner, from the aisles of 7-Eleven to shops tucked away inside massive office towers—is ramen.

It can be daunting, eating ramen in Japan for the first time, but after you've done it once, you'll be going back again and again for another bowl of steaming-hot, umami-rich broth piled high with toppings and noodles.

Ramen shops are a casual affair. Even the Michelin-starred ramen-ya are democratic: no reservations, no pretense, just good noodles. Your ramen adventure will most likely begin with a line, especially if you've chosen a popular place, but it'll move quickly—the ordering and seating process is streamlined. Once you get to the front of the line, a staff member will ask you to come into the shop to order.

Ramen vending machines can be difficult to decipher. Sometimes they'll have pictures of all the different bowls, but confusingly, all the bowls of noodles will look the same. If everything's in Japanese and you're not sure, pick the top left button; that's the spot where most ramen shops put their signature bowl. Slide your money in, watch the buttons light up, punch the button, then collect your ticket and change. Hand the ticket over to the staff, sit down where they tell you, and wait for noodle nirvana.

When your bowl of ramen arrives, dig in. Take a picture if you must, but don't take too long—the longer you wait, the softer the noodles get, and soft noodles are a tragedy. Ideally you'll start eating within 30 seconds; otherwise be prepared to get a subtle judge-y side-eye. Grab a twirl of noodles and slurp with abandon. When it comes to eating ramen, slurping is a superior method: As the noodles are pulled up through the piping-hot stock, they cool down just enough. When you're done, feel free to finish off the broth by picking up the bowl with both hands and drinking straight from it. Yell out a cheery *goshisosama* ("it was delicious"/"thank you for the meal"), and go on your merry way, content and full of noodles.

This recipe—which combines a Tokyo-style creamy chicken broth and a more northern Japanese-style miso-mushroom tare—embodies everything we love about ramen in one bowl. It's a richly flavored, super creamy, thick-bodied soup with a bit of the sea from the dashi and huge hits of umami from the miso, mushrooms, and chicken. It might feel excessive to buy both red and white miso, but it's the combination of the two that really makes this ramen shine. This recipe calls for just broth and noodles. If you want the full-on ramen experience, you'll need to prepare the chashu and ramen egg beforehand.

MISO AND MUSHROOMS

SUPER CREAMY CHICKEN MISO RAMEN

2 pounds chicken bones or 1 pound chicken wings

1 medium onion, halved

2 tablespoons (¼ stick) unsalted butter

¼ cup white miso

¼ cup red miso

2 tablespoons cooking sake

2 tablespoons mirin

2 tablespoons rice vinegar

1 ounce dried porcini mushrooms

2 cups dashi (see page 236)

Salt

24 ounces fresh ramen noodles

4 teaspoons peeled, grated fresh ginger (about a 1-inch piece)

4 cloves garlic, peeled and pressed or minced

½ medium red onion, peeled and finely minced

Finely sliced green onions

Chicken chashu (see page 217) and/or ramen egg (see page 217), for serving

1. Bring the chicken bones, onion, and 2 quarts of water to a boil in a large stockpot over high heat. Note the level of the water in the pot—you want to end up with this much liquid when the broth is done. Add an additional 2 quarts of water and keep it at a rolling boil for 2 hours, adding water as needed whenever the liquid drops below the original waterline.

2. Make the miso tare: Combine the butter, white and red miso, sake, mirin, vinegar, and mushrooms in a large saucepan and whisk over medium heat until the butter melts and the alcohol burns off, 1 to 2 minutes. Whisk in the dashi until smooth, then set aside.

3. When the chicken broth is done, remove it from the heat, strain, and discard the bones and onion. Pour the broth back into the pot. Add the miso tare to the broth and adjust the seasoning with salt to taste. Return the broth to very low heat and keep at a bare simmer.

4. Cook the noodles according to the package directions. Drain well.

5. To assemble: Ladle 2 cups of piping-hot ramen broth into each of four warmed bowls. Divide the noodles, ginger, garlic, red onion, and green onions among the bowls. Add the chicken chashu and/or ramen egg, and serve immediately.

Serves 4

Toppings

Marinated vegetables (we like to use bamboo shoots, baby corn, and wood ear mushrooms for this dish; see page 215)
Korean chili threads
Nori sheets

Porchetta—Italian roast pork that's rolled and stuffed with garlic, fennel, and rosemary—was the inspiration for this seriously good pasta. Since the meat in this dish is chopped, we skipped the classic rolling of the pork and instead focused on the crispy skin. For the ultimate in crunch, lightly score the skin, being careful not to cut all the way through to the meat. The scoring allows fat to be released slowly during roasting, leaving the skin crisp and crunchy. We contrasted the richness of the porchetta with a bright and fresh green sauce. This dish tastes like a lazy late-summer afternoon spent in Italy with your best friends.

PORCHETTA UNROLLED

REALLY CRISPY PORCHETTA WITH ZITI

1 pound skin-on pork belly

2 teaspoons fennel seeds, crushed

2 teaspoons flaky sea salt, plus extra as needed

1 teaspoon freshly cracked black pepper, plus extra as needed

½ cup first-press olive oil (see page 238)

2 cups loosely packed fresh flat-leaf parsley sprigs

¼ cup finely grated Parmigiano-Reggiano cheese

1 teaspoon coriander seeds, crushed

2 cloves garlic, peeled and pressed or minced

Finely grated zest and juice of 1 lemon

12 ounces dried ziti

1. Preheat your oven to 275°F.

2. Pat the pork belly dry with paper towels and lightly score or poke a bunch of holes in the skin with the tip of a sharp paring knife. Try not to go deeper than ¹⁄₁₆ inch.

3. Mix together 1 teaspoon of the fennel seeds, 2 teaspoons of flaky sea salt, and 1 teaspoon of black pepper in a small bowl. Rub the mixture all over the pork belly to coat it, then place it skin side up on a wire rack set in a deep roasting pan and roast until cooked through (the internal temperature of the pork should reach 160°F on an instant-read meat thermometer), about 1½ hours.

4. Meanwhile, make the green sauce by combining the remaining 1 teaspoon of fennel seeds with the oil, parsley, Parmigiano, coriander seeds, garlic, and lemon zest and juice in a blender, pulsing until smooth. Set it aside.

5. Once the pork is cooked through, turn the oven temperature up to 450°F and continue to roast, keeping an eye on the skin, until it is golden brown and crispy, 20 to 25 minutes. Remove it from the oven and let it rest for 15 minutes, then chop it into bite-size pieces.

6. Bring a large pot of salted water to a boil over high heat. Add the ziti and cook according to the package directions. Drain well, reserving 1 cup of the pasta cooking water.

7. In a large skillet over medium heat, briefly toss the pasta with the green sauce until the sauce warms up, about 1 minute. If the pasta seems dry, add pasta water 1 tablespoon at a time until the sauce is glossy. Season with salt and pepper to taste, then top with the pork belly. Serve, making sure everyone gets a bit of crispy crackling.

Serves 4

Toppings

Finely grated Parmigiano
Finely grated lemon zest
Crushed red pepper flakes

5x Better

Boost the flavors by lightly toasting the fennel and coriander seeds in a dry pan before crushing them.

tip!

Crispy roasted pork skin can be hard to cut if your knife isn't heavy and razor-sharp. To make the process easier, turn the pork skin side down. You can cut through the meat easily, then use the flat of your hand to push the knife through the skin safely.

XO SAUCE

SURF AND TURF IN A JAR

XO sauce is an addictive umami-rich mix of dried seafood, spice, and Chinese sausage that you can drizzle liberally on everything from vegetables to dumplings to noodles. It's deeply complex, layered, and quietly spicy, and it tastes like the ocean in the best way possible. It's all the flavors of surf and turf, in a jar, intensified.

You can buy decent XO sauce online or at any Asian grocery store. But if you're taking the trouble to source the sauce, the better option is to just buy the necessary ingredients from the same place and make your own.

This XO sauce recipe is a game changer. Unlike most XO sauce recipes, which require that you stand by the stove and stir, our recipe uses the oven to cook, concentrate, and caramelize. It's the easiest XO sauce recipe in the world. The low oven temp helps the dried seafood and aromatics slowly confit in oil, deepening in color and flavor. The result is a sauce you'll want to eat on everything.

THE EASIEST XO SAUCE

1 ounce dried scallops
(see page 237)

1 ounce dried shrimp
(see page 237)

1½ tablespoons Shaoxing
wine (see page 235)

3 shallots, peeled and
roughly chopped

6 cloves garlic, peeled
and pressed or minced

2 Thai chilies, seeded

1 link Chinese sausage,
roughly chopped

¾ cup neutral oil

1 tablespoon Chinese
chili flakes or crushed
red pepper flakes

1 teaspoon light soy
sauce

1 teaspoon sugar

1. Bring 1 cup of water to a boil in a small saucepan over
high heat.

2. Place the scallops and shrimp in a heatproof bowl
and combine with the Shaoxing wine and enough of the
boiling water to cover (discard the rest of the water).
Let the seafood soak for 30 minutes. Preheat your
oven to 300°F.

3. Drain the shrimp and scallops and place in a food
processor along with the shallots, garlic, chilies, and
Chinese sausage. Pulse until finely minced.

4. Heat ½ cup of the oil in a small, deep, ovenproof
saucepan over medium-high heat until an instant-read
thermometer reads 300°F.

5. Remove the saucepan from the heat and carefully stir
the seafood mixture into the oil. Place the saucepan in the
oven and bake, uncovered, stirring occasionally, until
the sauce is deeply caramelized and brown, 1 to 2 hours.

6. Remove the sauce from the oven and carefully stir
in the remaining ¼ cup of oil and the chili flakes, soy
sauce, and sugar. Let cool completely, transfer to a jar,
cover tightly, and refrigerate. The sauce will keep for
1 to 2 months.

Makes 1 cup

XO sauce is an instant umami booster. It tastes excellent as is, but when paired with butter and soy, its flavors really sing. Salty, spicy, and deeply delicious, this dish is one of our weeknight go-tos. It's super simple; this recipe is included in this chapter only because we really feel that the best XO sauce is the one you make yourself (see page 224). The ingredients we use to sauce the pasta—XO sauce, soy sauce, and butter—are immensely flavorful, so even though the sauce may not look like enough for the pasta, it's just right. Feel free to add vegetables and proteins as you wish—these noodles are completely customizable.

I Love You Like XO

TAGLIATELLE TOSSED WITH HOMEMADE XO SAUCE

Serves 4

Toppings

Chili oil (preferably homemade; page 53)
Crispy fried onions (page 239)
Sliced green onions
Chopped fresh cilantro

Salt

24 ounces fresh tagliatelle (preferably homemade; see page 14)

2 tablespoons (¼ stick) unsalted butter

½ cup XO sauce (preferably homemade, page 225)

2 tablespoons light soy sauce

1. Bring a large pot of salted water to a boil over high heat. Add the tagliatelle and cook until it just starts to float, 2 to 3 minutes. Drain well, reserving 1½ cups of the pasta cooking water.

2. Meanwhile, melt the butter in a large sauté pan over medium heat. Add the XO sauce and soy sauce, then ¾ cup of the pasta water, and whisk until the sauce emulsifies and comes to a gentle boil, 1 to 2 minutes.

3. Add the drained tagliatelle to the pan and cook gently, adding tablespoons of the pasta water as needed, until the pasta is al dente and the sauce reduces and becomes thick and glossy, about 1 minute. Serve immediately.

BIANG BIANG

If you've eaten at Xi'an Famous Foods in New York, you know what biang biang noodles are: handmade thick, wide, chewy noodle goodness. The actual birthplace of biang biang noodles is in central China, in Shaanxi province. They used to be more of a peasant-type noodle, but now they're pretty much ubiquitous in Shaanxi and especially in Xi'an, the capital. There are a bunch of theories on the name—that it comes from the sound the noodles make when you bang them on the table or the sound that people make when they eat the noodles—and even more theories on why the Chinese character for biang is so complex (it's made up of 58 strokes).

But really, all you need to know about biang biang noodles is that they're good. They're hearty and hold up well when fried, tossed, and added to soups. We even like to go a little crazy and use them where you'd typically use pasta.

Use these noodles wherever you want a fresh chewy noodle. They go exceptionally well in Chinese Bolognese (page 91), Taiwanese beef noodle soup (page 143), or dan dan (page 95). Or try them simply tossed with Spicy Sichuan Wonton Chili Sauce (page 165), XO sauce (page 225), or even traditional Bolognese (page 201)—it's next-level. Note that these noodles are meant to be cooked as soon as you make them, so plan accordingly.

HAND-PULLED

Biang Biang Noodles

10 ounces all-purpose
   flour (about 2⅓ cups)

¼ teaspoon salt

Neutral oil

**Makes 2 portions
of noodles**

tip!

Keep a small bowl of
oil around to dip your
hands into while you're
shaping the noodles.

   If you want to skip
the hand-pulling, you
can just roll out the
dough to your desired
thickness and cut it into
your desired noodle
width with a sharp
knife.

1. Use a pair of chopsticks to stir together the flour and salt in a large bowl. Slowly add ½ cup of water, stirring until the mixture comes together into a shaggy dough. Turn the dough out onto a clean work surface and knead until the dough is smooth, elastic, and not at all sticky, about 20 minutes. If the dough is too dry, add water, a teaspoon at a time. Alternatively, you can use a dough hook and a stand mixer on low speed.

2. Form the dough into a ball and wrap it in lightly oiled plastic wrap. Let it rest at room temperature for at least 2 hours and up to 24 hours. (It's best if you can make this the day before and let it rest overnight—the dough will have lots of hands-off time to develop gluten, making the noodles thick and chewy.)

3. When you're ready to pull the noodles, lightly oil the dough and divide it into halves. Cover one portion with plastic wrap while you work with the other one. Lightly oil your work surface and a tray. Place the dough on the work surface and roll it into a rectangle about ¼ inch thick. Use a knife to cut it into 1-inch-wide strips. Cover the strips with plastic wrap.

4. Working with one dough strip at a time, use the heel of your hand to flatten it into a very wide, long strip, then take hold of both ends of the strip and bang it against the oiled work surface, pulling your hands apart slowly so that you're stretching the dough. There's no trick to pulling the noodles—as long as your dough has rested enough and you slowly stretch out your hands, the dough will comply. Pull until the noodle is 20 to 24 inches long and about ⅛ inch thick. Lay the noodle on your prepared tray (you may need to snake the noodle to fit) and cover with plastic wrap so it doesn't dry out. Repeat with the remaining dough until it is used up.

5. Bring a large pot of water to a boil over high heat. Add the noodles and stir gently so they don't stick to each other or the bottom of the pot. Cook until tender, chewy, and cooked through, 4 to 5 minutes. Drain well.

6. To serve, toss the noodles with the sauce of your choice, and enjoy.

We often play a game where we rate our top 10s, and we always struggle with rating our top 10 bites. There are just too many good options. But we always agree when it comes to this dish: These smoky, savory, chewy, flavorful, spicy noodles are absolutely one of the best bites we've ever eaten.

Toasting the spices gently draws out their nuttiness and citrus undertones while adding a mellow complexity. Cooking the lamb in small batches ensures that you have the right amount of heat (a lot) to sear the meat.

KiSS KiSS BANG BANG

SMOKY CUMIN LAMB WITH BIANG BIANG NOODLES

2 tablespoons cumin seeds

1 tablespoon coriander seeds

2 tablespoons light soy sauce

1 teaspoon dark soy sauce

1 teaspoon Shaoxing wine (see page 235)

1 teaspoon cornstarch

1 tablespoon peeled and grated fresh ginger

4 cloves garlic, peeled and pressed or minced

½ pound boneless lamb shoulder or chuck, very thinly sliced

2 tablespoons chili oil (preferably homemade; page 53)

2 teaspoons Chinese black vinegar (see page 235)

1 batch Hand-Pulled Biang Biang Noodles (page 229)

Neutral oil, for stir-frying

½ small red onion, peeled and sliced

2 ribs celery, cut into 1-inch strips

1. Toast the cumin and coriander seeds in a small dry pan over medium-low heat, shaking the pan until they start to smell fragrant and toasty, 1 to 2 minutes. Let cool, then crush using a mortar and pestle.

2. Combine 1 teaspoon of the spice mixture with 1 tablespoon of light soy sauce and the dark soy sauce, Shaoxing wine, cornstarch, ginger, and garlic in a medium bowl. Add the lamb and stir well to coat. Marinate at room temperature for 1 hour.

3. Make the sauce by combining the remaining spice mixture with the remaining 1 tablespoon of light soy sauce, the chili oil, and the black vinegar in a small bowl. Set aside.

4. Bring a large pot of water to a boil over high heat. Add the noodles and stir gently so they don't stick to each other or the bottom of the pot. Cook until tender, chewy, and cooked through, 4 to 5 minutes. Drain well and set aside.

5. Heat a large wok or conventional (not nonstick) skillet over high heat. Just as the wok starts to smoke, add 1 tablespoon of neutral oil. Add half of the lamb and its marinade and stir-fry until deeply browned, 5 to 6 minutes, then remove and set aside. Add more oil if needed. Once the oil is smoking, sear the remaining lamb until deeply browned, then remove from the wok and set aside with the first batch.

6. Add the red onion and celery to the wok and stir-fry until the vegetables are tender-crisp, about 1 minute. Add the drained noodles, lamb, and sauce to the pan and toss until everything is evenly coated. Serve immediately.

Serves 2

Toppings
Chili oil
Sliced green onions
Toasted sesame seeds

tip!

The chili oil you use here is key, so if you don't go with homemade, take your time finding a store-bought chili oil that you love. If you want to add an extra dimension of flavor, stir a teaspoon of sugar into the sauce in Step 3. It'll give the whole dish a sweet and spicy feel.

Ingredients

Good Noodles Need Good Ingredients

Finding and buying the right ingredients is half the battle when you're cooking. When a recipe calls for only four to six ingredients, missing or substituting even one can change the taste of the final dish. Of course, there's room for flexibility within a recipe and you can riff on it as you need to—the information in the following section will explain what's what in our recipes and how to make substitutions in a pinch. For those other times when a specific brand or type of ingredient is highly recommended, we've included our favorites.

One last note on ingredients: For an automatic flavor upgrade, try buying a small size of the more expensive imported varieties of canned and bottled items, like fish and olive oils, rather than buying a larger bottle of the "cheap" stuff. It's hard to step out of our comfort zone and buy the seemingly overpriced versions of things, but the boost in flavor is usually worth it.

Oils, Vinegars, and Alcohols

① Sesame Oil

In this book, when we say sesame oil, we exclusively mean the very dark toasted stuff that's usually found in the Asian foods aisle. Toasted sesame oil is used extensively in Asian cuisine as a flavoring oil, adding a deep, rich, toasty hit of sesame to anything and everything. Our favorite brand is Kadoya.

② Sake

Sake is one of the backbones of Japanese cuisine, and unlike wine, any brand of sake is fine for cooking—including the very cheap cooking sake sold in the Asian aisle at the grocery store, which is what we use. You can also find it online.

③ Rice Vinegar

When we say rice vinegar, we're referring to Japanese rice vinegar. It's acidic, delicate, mild, and slightly sweet. Go for the unseasoned one; the seasoned one is mainly for sushi rice. It's available in the Asian food aisle in most grocery stores, at Asian grocery stores, and online.

④ Shaoxing Wine

Shaoxing is a Chinese fermented rice wine that adds depth and complexity and that subtle difference between your average home-cooked Chinese food and high-end Chinese restaurant food. Try to choose an unsalted wine—it should have subtle nutty notes of vinegar and caramel without being overwhelming. Pagoda brand is our favorite and is what we use in the recipes throughout the book; make sure you season to taste if you're using a different brand. You can find it in the Asian foods aisle, at an Asian grocery store, and online. Pale dry sherry will work as a substitute in a pinch.

⑤ Mirin

Along with soy sauce, sake, and dashi, mirin is a cornerstone ingredient in Japanese cooking. Subtly sweet and slightly tangy, mirin adds round notes and a richness that make it an essential ingredient for almost all Japanese recipes. Find it in the Asian foods aisle in a supermarket, at an Asian grocery store, and online.

⑥ Chinese Black Vinegar

Chinese black vinegar, also called Chinkiang vinegar, is made from a black sticky rice that has a deep flavor with a hint of smoke. The resulting vinegar is malty, slightly sweet, and just a little bit reminiscent of balsamic—perfect for balancing out soups and sauces. It's available in the Asian food aisle, at Asian grocery stores, and online.

⑦ Soy Sauce

We could write a whole chapter on soy sauce. Most good Asian grocery stores devote a whole aisle to the hundreds of different types. Basically, though, there are two main varieties commercially available: naturally brewed/fermented and chemically produced. Get the naturally brewed or fermented for its complex deep aroma and flavor. We like both Amoy and Lee Kum Kee brands for Chinese recipes and Yamasa or Kikkoman for Japanese and Korean ones. When it comes to Chinese soy sauces, you're looking for a darker, dense, salty finish that lends itself well to the robust flavors of Chinese dishes. Japanese soy has a lighter, sweeter, rounder profile, which pairs well with the subtle flavors of Japanese food as well as the punchier flavors of Korean. If you have space in your pantry, get a bottle of Chinese dark soy sauce, too—it adds color and a hint of caramel and salt. Add a teaspoon or two to stir-fried noodles for an extra glossy brown sheen and hit of umami.

8 Chinese Sesame Paste

Chinese sesame paste is made with whole toasted seeds and is thicker than tahini. It has an intensely toasted flavor and deep color. In a pinch, you can substitute tahini mixed with toasted sesame oil (use 1 teaspoon of toasted sesame oil for every tablespoon of tahini). Chinese sesame paste is available at Asian grocery stores and online.

9 Dashi

An umami-forward Japanese stock made from kombu and bonito flakes, dashi is the base flavor layer of almost all Japanese dishes. Making it from scratch is kind of like making tea: kombu and bonito (or one or more other dried fishes) are steeped in hot-but-not-boiling water. Bring 4 cups of water to a boil, remove from the heat, and add a 4 x 4-inch piece of kombu along with 1 cup of high-quality bonito flakes. Let steep for 10 minutes, then strain. For a shortcut, pick up dashi "tea bags"; they are super simple to use and you should be able to find them at any Asian grocery store or online. Our favorite brand is Kayanoya, an artisanal brand from Kyushu that is available online.

10 Kimchi

Kimchi needs no introduction, but the brand you use can impart a huge difference in taste. We like the Korean brands Tobagi and Chongga. American kimchi is often just as good, but why not go right to the source? Kimchi is available in the refrigerated section near the tofu at most supermarkets, at Asian grocery stores, and online.

11 Oyster Sauce

Contrary to popular belief, real oyster sauce really does have oysters in it. Lee Kum Kee invented oyster sauce in 1888, and it's our brand of choice. They have two versions: one with a boat on the label and another one with a panda. If you look closely, the panda bottle is half the price and is "oyster flavored." Choose the bottle with the boat. It's available in the Asian foods aisle, at an Asian grocery store, and online.

12 Hoisin Sauce

Fermented soybeans are cooked down with sugar and vinegar to create the thick, sweet, and rich umami bomb known as hoisin sauce. You can get hoisin just about anywhere these days, but we prefer Lee Kum Kee (the squeeze-bottle version, for ease). It's available in the Asian aisle in most grocery stores, at an Asian grocery store, and online.

13 Parmigiano-Reggiano

Cheese names in America are not restricted by law; anyone can call their cheese Parmesan—which means the quality of Parmesan can be all over the map. We prefer the real stuff from Italy, Parmigiano-Reggiano, which has a laser-imprinted rind telling you exactly what kind of cheese it is. Made from cow's milk, Parmigiano is made in only two regions in northern Italy and is aged for at least one year. It's called the King of Cheeses for its addictive nutty, sharp flavor. It adds a big hit of umami to sauces and is the perfect finishing cheese.

14 Pecorino Romano

Pecorino is the lesser-known little brother who doesn't get as much love as big brother Parmigiano. Really though, pecorino is an unsung hero: Intense and salty, pecorino is perfect for pasta recipes, both in the sauces and as a finishing cheese. Real pecorino Romano, much like Parmigiano-Reggiano, will have a laser-imprinted rind. Made in central Italy, this hard cheese is made from sheep's milk and aged for five to eight months.

15 Gochujang

Traditionally sold in red plastic tubs, gochujang is a Korean staple: a bright red, fermented, thick and sticky hot pepper paste that adds a savory, sweet, spicy hit of flavor. Different brands have different heat levels, so be sure to look at the label for a heat scale indicator and choose accordingly. It's available in the Asian foods aisle, at Asian grocery stores, and online.

16 Miso

Miso is to Japan what Parmigiano-Reggiano is to Italy. It's a nationally prized source of umami created with not much more than fermented soybeans, salt, and koji (a mold). Miso comes in two major varieties: white, which is young and light, and red, which is aged and strong. Chefs have been known to drive across the Japanese countryside searching for artisanal miso with just the right taste for their dishes. Here we don't have that luxury, but blending red and white miso produces a wonderful mix of umami that's more than adequate for making ramen, miso soup (mix 1 tablespoon each of red and white miso with 2 cups of dashi), and any other miso-forward dishes you can think of (we like to heat up equal parts red and white miso with Parmigiano over medium-low heat and toss that with pasta water and pasta).

17 Fish Sauce

It was only after years of creating recipes and getting questions on our blog about fish sauce that we realized that many people don't know there are two kinds—clear and opaque. Opaque fish sauce is fermented and can smell really potent. In this book, we only use the clear fish sauce. Like olive oil, the best fish sauce comes from the first pressing; look for "first pressed" or "mam nhi" on the label. You can find fish sauce in the Asian foods aisle, at Asian grocery stores, and online.

18 Doubanjiang

Doubanjiang is made from a blend of chilies and fermented soy and broad beans. Look for a package that lists beans and chili peppers as the main ingredients. If you can't find authentic doubanjiang, Lee Kum Kee makes a Cantonese-style version labeled Toban Djan. Look for either style at an Asian grocery store or online.

19 Bonito Flakes

Bonito flakes are the shavings of a bonito fish that's been smoked and dried. They taste and smell just like the best smoked fish you've ever had. The quality of bonito flakes can vary greatly. In Japan, it's possible to buy a whole block of bonito and a plane to shave it yourself. The cheap stuff you find in the Asian aisle of most supermarkets (if you can even find any) is actually the odds and ends and dust left over from making higher-quality bonito flakes. Look for 1-inch-wide shavings in large bags imported from Japan, usually at Japanese/Asian supermarkets or online.

20 Kombu

Kombu is dried kelp/seaweed, and it smells like the sea in the best possible way. It's not really possible to be too picky about the kombu you can find outside of Japan, but thankfully it's all generally of pretty good quality. The Shirakiku brand of dashi kombu is widely available everywhere and it's often what we use when we run out of whatever we've brought back from Tokyo. Don't bring kombu to a boil; always steep it in water that's come off the boil and off the heat, or else it'll develop bitter notes.

21 Dried Seafood

Dried seafood adds an extra boost of complex, concentrated ocean umami. Essentially, it's seafood that's been sun-dried for an intense, rich flavor. We use two kinds of dried seafood in this book: shrimp and scallops. Both need to be reconstituted by soaking in hot water. When buying dried seafood, it's best to hop on over to an Asian grocery store so you can get a good look at what you're buying. You want not-too-dry, oily, plump, light pinkish-orange guys; size isn't really a factor for most of our dishes. For the less common dried scallops especially, the larger they are, the more expensive they will be; small scallops are preferable for our purposes because they're sweeter and flake more easily. The best dried scallops are from Japan. If you can't find them locally, look for them online.

22 Chinese Chili Flakes

Chinese Sichuan chili flakes are a vibrant bright red and don't have as many seeds in them as Italian-style crushed red pepper flakes. Chinese flakes are made by frying whole chilies in oil until crispy, then grinding the pods into flakes, giving them a nice nutty flavor and texture. They're perfect in chili oil or as a finishing touch. They're available at Asian grocery stores and online.

23 Crispy Fried Shallots and Onions

Crispy fried shallots and onions are two of our favorite noodle toppings, both for pastas and for Asian noodles. You could break out the oil and deep-fry these at home, but we find it much easier and tastier to just pick up a container from the Asian grocery store or even IKEA. They add just the right amount of addictive crunch and salty onion-y flavor. Technically onions and shallots are two different things, but let's be honest here: They taste like deep-fried goodness, and we're not picky. They're like sprinkles but for savories.

24 Guanciale

Italian cured pork cheeks might be the best bacon you've ever tasted. The robust flavor from guanciale comes from both the fat and the seasonings rubbed on the surface before curing. The flavors are super concentrated but not too salty, and when rendered, the fat is fragrant, sweet, and savory. Guanciale is what Italians use for their carbonara, amatriciana, and alla gricia. It's sold whole, which is perfect for cutting into whatever size cubes you need. Sub pancetta if guanciale is nowhere to be found. It's available at specialty stores, good butcher shops, and online.

25 Olive and Neutral Oils (not pictured)

In this book we use olive and neutral oil for general cooking. There's a huge amount of olive oil available, but for our purposes we use two: regular olive oil (sometimes called light or pure) and a nice high-quality first-press olive oil. Regular olive oil is lighter in color and taste compared with first press. For finishing, we always reach for the first-press olive oil. It's fruity, robust, and full of flavor.

Neutral oil is the workhorse of our kitchen. When choosing a neutral oil, we look for something with an extremely high smoke point and as little flavor as possible. At home, this always means grapeseed oil, but when we are traveling and can't be as picky, we also like safflower oil, rice bran oil, sunflower oil, or canola oil.

Equipment for Your Noodle Kitchen

If You Hate Cooking, It's OK to Blame Your Tools

It's often repeated that you don't need that much stuff in the kitchen, that you should avoid single-use gadgets, or that you should just outfit kitchens with cheap and serviceable equipment, ideally from a restaurant supply store. While that's good advice, sometimes a well-made or luxury piece of equipment can change your cooking life, especially when it comes to noodles. We can't imagine making homemade pasta without a pasta roller, and likewise, we can't imagine cooking without thermometers, scales, and specialty ladles and scoops. If you can justify the cost of some of these items, they'll make cooking a pure pleasure rather than a chore.

Equipment So Essential That It Travels with Us

This isn't a complete list of everything you need in a kitchen; it's more of a list of things that will make cooking easy, effortless, and fun. We consider this equipment so essential, we carry it in our luggage when we travel.

① Knives: 1 good knife, 1 bad knife, and a sharpener

The common wisdom is that you only need three knives: a bread knife, a chef's knife, and a paring knife. Throughout our cooking life, we've found that while it's nice to have those options, all we *really* need is one good knife, one bad knife, and a sharpener to keep them both as sharp as possible. The good knife is the difference between easy dicing and angrily calling for pizza. The bad knife is there so you don't abuse your good knife. Chefs around the world know that when you need to hack through some bones, you use the shop knife, never your good one. For either knife, you don't want to go too short, but you also don't need to go too long. For us, the ideal blade length for our main knives is around 7 inches. The reason you shouldn't go too long is that it's important to feel comfortable with both the middle and the tip of your knife. For knives of all sorts, we like Henckels, especially their Japanese collections, which come from Seki.

Originally a village in Japan, Seki is now a small city of 90,000 that has been making blades of all sorts for hundreds of years and continues the tradition to this day. Japanese blades tend to be thinner and lighter and made with a sharper bevel than their Western variants. Knives are always a personal thing, and you should use what works best for you, but anyone who cooks often should give a high-quality carbon steel knife a serious audition.

② Garlic Press

A solid garlic press is a one-stop garlic solution. Sure, you can just practice your knife skills and mince garlic to your heart's content, but when you are doing 10+ cloves of garlic, these things are lifesavers. We find it's easier to peel garlic by crushing the clove partway to break the peel and remove it by hand rather than pressing the clove with the peel intact, which makes the press harder to clean. Either way, choose a press that's dishwasher-safe and comes with a scraper to remove the leftover bits easily.

③ Instant-Read Thermometer

Cooking is about temperature control, and if you don't have a reliable way of understanding temperature, you're basically blind. Gone are the days of using your palm or ear to figure out the doneness of steaks; now we know exactly what temperature we would like our steak to reach. There are lots of great reasonably priced instant-read thermometers online. You're looking for something that has an accuracy within 1°F and a read time of under 10 seconds. A good thermocouple-type thermometer will typically have a read time of around 3 seconds, will be very accurate, and shouldn't cost more than $20.

④ Scale

Given how cheap a digital scale is, it is an amazingly helpful cooking tool. We bought ours originally for baking, but time and time again we turn to it for any type of cooking you can think of. When shopping for a scale, look for one with a precision of 0.1 gram and an auto-off feature that isn't too aggressive; nothing is more frustrating than losing your weight reading in the middle of cooking. We have multiple accurate, affordable scales we bought online for cheap.

⑤ Tongs and Strainers

A good set of tongs is a no-brainer, and for noodles a sieve or strainer spoon is even better. Ours comes from Japan, but Joseph Joseph makes one sold everywhere that's largely identical and will make your life so much easier. For delicate noodles, silicone-covered tongs are a must.

Luxuries

These are the things that we've splurged on and never regretted. They make life easier and more fun, and they open up lots of new culinary doors but aren't strictly essential. If your budget allows, consider some of these items.

1. Pasta Roller

Beyond actually rolling pasta, a pasta roller is a great at-home substitute for a commercial noodle machine in that it can help you to knead otherwise unkneadable low-hydration noodle doughs such as udon or hakata-style ramen. Having tried many pasta machines in our noodle-making lives, we can confidently say that this is one piece of equipment where choosing a brand name makes a big difference. The expensive colorful Italian machines have tighter tolerances that will up your homemade noodle game. They're worth the extra investment over the cheap generic copies.

2. Timer

We own multiple timers and use them religiously. Timers allow your brain to move to other tasks without fear of forgetting what's on the stove. They enable you to cook multiple things simultaneously, making your cooking experience faster, easier, and less stressful.

3. Mortar and Pestle

A good mortar and pestle will change the way you cook. The mechanical act of crushing spices and aromatics opens up oils and flavor notes that you can't get any other way. Mortars and pestles come in both wood and stone forms. Traditionally you use the wood one when you want to crush dry ingredients and the stone one for wet, but we've found that just the wood one works fine for both. A neat trick we have is to use just a wooden pestle with a heavy set of ceramic mixing bowls. All of a sudden, you have a customizable mortar and pestle set that's good for crushing any amount of food.

4. Woks and Dutch Ovens

For cooking Asian food, a large wok—as large as you can handle with as round of a bottom as your stove can support—makes life a lot easier. Sometimes we even use ours for saucing pasta because there's nothing better suited to tossing food than a proper wok. The rest of the time, we use Dutch ovens, which can come very inexpensively and are dishwasher-, oven-, and high-temp safe. (Note: Dutch oven not shown to scale.)

5. Food Processor

It doesn't matter how good your knife skills are, sometimes it's easier and more fun just to throw everything in a food processor and blitz away. Plus, time saver!

6. Rasps and Large Microplanes

We grate all hard cheeses by hand using a large, wide Microplane fine grater. It grates hard cheese like no other, producing fine cheesy strands. We also love the rough rasps (i.e., the smallest holes on a four-sided box grater) that turn cheese into a pile of fluffy snow, kind of like the stuff that comes out of a green can, but real and fresh.

7. Dishwasher-Safe Cutting Boards

We own a fancy Boos Block for guests to ooh and ahh over, but when we're cooking a dozen recipes a day, we always reach for our heavy-duty, dishwasher-safe, poly cutting boards with nonslip feet. Having more than one really changes the game, and we've settled on four as a good number—but we cook for a living. Having even just two can make your cooking life so much easier.

8. Whisks

A wire whisk (like this itty-bitty one) is our favorite tool to reach for when we want to aerate and smooth out sauces. We use them for perfectly lump-free mac and cheese, besciamella, and cornstarch slurries. They are also perfect for whisking pasta water into sauces.

9. Offset Spatulas

If you look into our dishwasher after we've spent a long day cooking, you might be surprised to find a row of dirtied-up mini offset spatulas waiting for a wash. We reach for them again and again. Their thin, flexible offset blade is perfect for sliding underneath and lifting food, and running alongside the edges of lasagna pans to release all that cheesy baked goodness.

Index

Note: Page references in *italics* indicate photographs.

Mushroom(s):
    and kale lasagna, 186, *187*
    like fondue but it's Korean army
        stew, 108, *109*
    super creamy chicken miso ramen,
        220, 221
Mussels:
    casarecce moules frites–hold the
        frites, 92, *93*
Mustard:
    garlic miso, 88, *88*
    lemon honey, 88, *88*

N
Neutral oil, about, 239
Noodle bowls:
    dressings for, 88, *88*
    formula for, 86
    proteins and vegetables for,
        89, *89*
Noodles:
    adding to boiling water, xiv
    Asian, xiv
    cooking times, xiv
    definition of, ix
    draining, xv
    eating right away, xvi
    fresh vs. dried vs. frozen, xiii
    precooked, soaking, xv
    rinsing, xv
    seasoning and saucing, xix
    spicy sesame chili oil, 54, *55*
    substituting, notes on, ix–xi
    toppings for, xvi
    see also specific types
Noodle soups:
    bowls for, xv
    bun bo hue, about, 77
    the noodle soup you never knew you
        loved, *80*, 81
    super savory Taiwanese beef,
        143–45, *144*
    topping ideas for, 78, *79*
    warming bowls for, xv–xvi
    weeknight chipotle adobo pork belly
        ramen, 168–69, *169*
    wonton, like they do in HKG,
        166, *167*
    see also Laksa; Pho

O
Olive oil, about, 239
Onion(s):
    crispy fried, about, 239
    green, oil chow mein, 40, *41*
    mac and cheese, French, 22, *23*
    ramen with slow-braised pork belly
        kimchi stew, *118*, 119
Oven-roasted yakiudon al pastor,
    102, 103–4
Over-the-top Bolognese with
    handmade pappardelle, *200*,
    201–2
Oyster sauce, about, 236
Oyster sauce, garlic-butter bucatini
    with, 42, *43*

P
Pappardelle, xi, 14, *15*
    Chinese Bolognese, 90, *91*
    handmade, over-the-top Bolognese
        with, *200*, 201–2
Pasta:
    cooking al dente, xiv
    eating right away, xvi
    fresh vs. dried vs. frozen, xiii
    homemade, with a chitarra, 12–14,
        13, *15*
    rinsing, xv
    salting water for, xiv
    seasoning and saucing, xix
    substituting, notes on, ix–xi
    see also specific types
Peas and slow-braised lamb with
    reginette, 105–7, *106*
Penne, giant, with crispy guanciale,
    30, *31*
Peppers:
    Philly cheesesteak instant mazemen,
        64, *65*
    rib eye with black bean sauce and
        crispy chow mein, 44, *45*
    see also Chile peppers
Philly cheesesteak instant mazemen,
    64, *65*
Pho:
    about, 137–38
    chicken, ultimate weeknight,
        146, *147*

roasted bone marrow and beef
    brisket, 140, 141–42
ultimate weeknight chicken pho,
    146, *147*
Pici, 14, *15*
Pici with lots of cheese and cracked
    black pepper, *16*, 17
Pineapple:
    oven-roasted yakiudon al pastor,
        102, 103–4
Pork:
    an even more ridiculous lasagna
        with meatballs inside, 192–94,
        193
    belly, slow-braised, kimchi stew,
        ramen with, *118*, 119
    belly and cracked black pepper fusilli
        bucati, *206*, 207
    belly and kale, fried Shanghai
        noodles with, 18, *19*
    belly ramen, weeknight chipotle
        adobo, 168–69, *169*
    Chinese BBQ, *130*, 130–31
    Chinese Bolognese pappardelle,
        90, *91*
    meatballs, charred, with vermicelli,
        124–25, *125*
    oven-roasted yakiudon al pastor,
        102, 103–4
    over-the-top Bolognese with
        handmade pappardelle, *200*,
        201–2
    pecorino, and chitarra, 8, *9*
    really crispy porchetta with ziti,
        222, 223
    and shrimp wontons, 163, *164*
    slow-braised sugo with tagliatelle,
        4, *5*
    spaghettoni and roasted garlic fennel
        meatballs, 32, 33–34
    spicy, Sichuan dan dan mian,
        94, *95*
    spicy Sichuan mapo tofu chitarra,
        208, *209*
    tomato sugo, creamy, lasagna with,
        188, 189
    the ultimate lasagna alla Bolognese,
        178–79, *179*
    see also Bacon; Guanciale; Sausage

About the Authors

Steph and Mike are authors, photographers, recipe developers, and noodle obsessives who have spent the last decade traveling full-time in the search of good food. Whether it's smoky green chile cheeseburgers in the deserts of New Mexico, authentic tagliatelle Bolognese in the hills of Bologna, perfect paella by the coast in Valencia, or silky Sanuki-style udon on the coast of Kagawa, there's nowhere they won't go for a dish—especially if it's noodle-based. Together, they're the husband-and-wife team behind *i am a food blog*, an award-winning blog about all things food and food-adjacent. *That Noodle Life* is their second cookbook.